Pinewood Derby®
Designs & Patterns

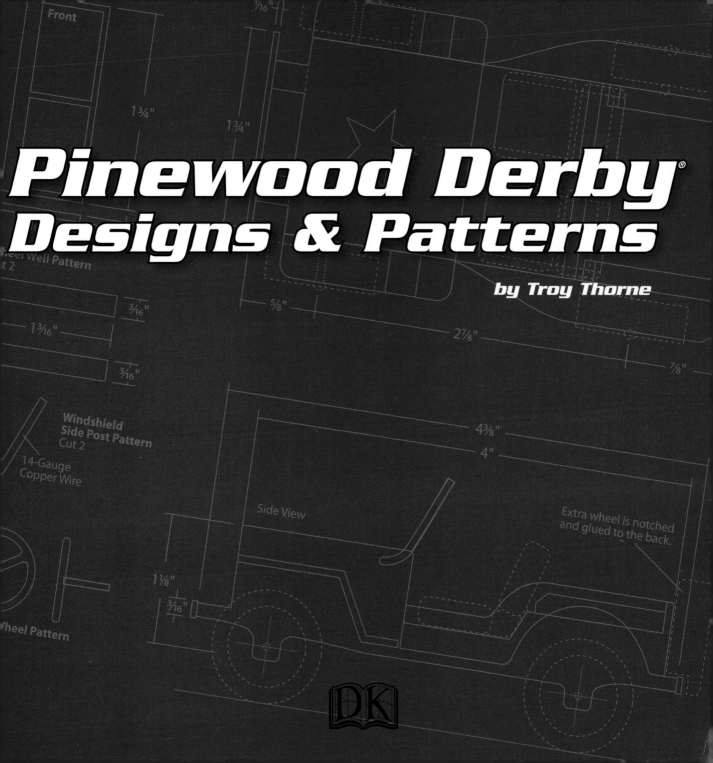

Pinewood Derby®
Designs & Patterns

by Troy Thorne

This title was designed and produced by Fox Chapel Publishing and distributed under a special arrangement by DK Publishing, an Official Licensee of Boy Scouts of America.

Fox Chapel Publishing
1970 Broad Street
East Petersburg, PA 17520

Alan Giagnocavo
President

J. McCrary
Publisher

Peg Couch
Concept Editor

Gretchen Bacon
Editor

Troy Thorne
Design and Layout

Scott Kriner/Troy Thorne
Photography

Pinewood Derby®, Cub Scouts®, and Boy Scouts of America® are registered trademarks of the Boy Scouts of America. Printed under license from Boy Scouts of America to DK Publishing.

ISBN: 978–0–7566–3262–5

Publisher's Cataloging-in-Publication Data
Thorne, Troy.

Pinewood Derby designs & patterns / by Troy Thorne. -- New York, NY : DK Publishing, c2007.
    p. : col. ill. ; cm.
    ISBN: 978-0-7566-3262-5
Summary: Learn the secrets to crafting cool cars for the Pinewood Derby. Includes designs, detailed measured drawings and cutting patterns, tips and techniques for peak performance and safety.

    1. Model car racing--United States. 2. Automobiles, Racing-- Models--Design and construction. 3. Cub Scouts--United States. I. Title. II. Title: Pinewood Derby designs and patterns.

GV1570 .T46 2007
796.15/6—dc22   0711

Printed in China
10 9 8 7 6 5 4 3 2 1

Boy Scouts of America encourages all scouts and their supporters to abide by the Scout Oath and Law when competing. Always check and follow your local Pinewood Derby's rules and regulations before you begin building your car. If you are unsure about what modifications are allowable, check with your local race organizer.

About the Author

Creative director, woodworker, and active Scouting volunteer Troy Thorne drew on his artistic roots and personal experience, as well as the experiences of other top Derby car designers, to create this book on cool designs for hot Derby cars. A graduate of Savannah College of Art and Design, Troy spent 10 years as senior art director for a large advertising agency before becoming creative director of Fox Chapel Publishing. He builds furniture and canoes in his spare time and participates in Scouting activities with his son, Nathan, who was a national finalist in the All-Star Derby Design Contest. Troy's latest project is a street-legal AC Cobra replica.

Table of Contents

Introduction

Even though speed is probably most Pinewood Derby® racers' top priority, the modifications you make for speed can leave you feeling unsure about how your car will perform until you actually race it. That's why, when my son and I made our first car together, we felt it needed to feature a cool design. Whether or not it won the prize for being the fastest, we knew we'd always have a car that looked great and that we could be proud of.

Our first car was almost as slow as we had feared, but it still won two trophies: Coolest Car and Scouts' Choice. Since then, we have built several cars that have won prizes for both speed and design. Our idea of making fast but attractive cars is the basis for this book. There is a lot to learn, so let's get started!

Building a car together

Spending time with your child is one of the most important aspects of participating in the Pinewood Derby. It's also important to be aware of what you and your child can learn from building a car together. Though some may seem obvious, following a few simple principles will help make the Pinewood Derby a truly rewarding experience for both of you.

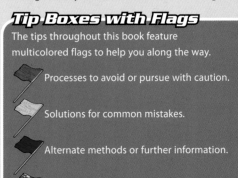

Our first car wasn't fast, but it won two prizes for outstanding design.

Work as a team. Find a way for your child to participate in every step of the process. The best way to accomplish this is to let him perform as many steps as possible. Teach by example whenever you can. For instance, you might show your child how to complete a step of the process on one side of the car and then allow him to do the same step on the other side of the car. If he is unable to complete the step by himself, assist him but be sure he participates as much as possible. Some steps must be performed by an adult for safety reasons. Even in these situations, try to find some way to safely involve your child in the work you do.

Whether or not he can perform a particular step, encourage your child to work closely by your side so he can see exactly what you are doing. You may want to provide something safe for him to stand on so he can be at your eye level. Ask questions, such as "Do both sides look even?" to help keep him focused on the task even if he isn't physically doing the work. The more steps your child understands and participates in, the more he will feel as if he is a part of the process.

Let your child help decide which body style to make. Your child will feel more connected to his car if you allow him to be creative and influence its design. This book provides several patterns for all skill levels. Look through the designs with your child and decide on one together.

Tip Boxes with Flags

The tips throughout this book feature multicolored flags to help you along the way.

Processes to avoid or pursue with caution.

Solutions for common mistakes.

Alternate methods or further information.

Speed tips.

Consider the level of woodworking experience needed before you commit to building a specific car. Also, review the tools and supplies you'll need for each body style before choosing.

Let your child pick the color and detail options. If he wants to add detail, such as a steering wheel, stickers, or decals, encourage him to express his creativity in this area. Allow him to place them on the car. Putting your child in charge of different aspects of the project shows him that you value his judgment.

Teach skills and techniques as you work. Building a Pinewood Derby car with your child is a great way to develop woodworking and math skills. Go over all of the tools and their uses with your child and help him understand how they work. When it's time to actually build the car, remember to teach by example and to allow your child to learn at his own pace. You might show him how to hold the coping saw and then let him make the cuts on the car by imitating the position and techniques you've demonstrated. Always encourage your child: Be quick with praise and downplay small mistakes.

Make it fun. The Pinewood Derby is a great opportunity for you and your child to create a special bond as you work together to build the car. Give yourself enough time so you and your child don't feel rushed or overwhelmed. Remember, building a Pinewood Derby car should be a fun experience for both of you.

How to use this book

This book is designed to allow anyone to create an attractive car, regardless of his or her level of experience. Chapter 1 covers general information on safety and on the various tools and supplies that you'll need to create a Derby car.

Chapter 2 includes how-to demonstrations for three designs, each of a different skill level. If you're making a Pinewood Derby car for the first time, the High-Wing

Racer is a simple but striking design that will help you build your skills. The Stock Car is a little more complex, requiring you to add wood to the initial block. The Vintage Racecar is the most complex design.

Once you have completed the car that best suits your skill level, you can move on to the painting section, which provides a number of different techniques for painting and detailing your Pinewood Derby car. Tips along the way help you avoid or fix common mistakes.

The book also features a pattern portfolio, which provides profiles and design ideas for all skill levels, measured drawings, cutting patterns and templates, tips, and reference photos. Once you have worked through your favorite designs in the book, use the blank block outlines to create your own designs.

Quick Tips list the best step-by-step method for building the car.

Reference photos show the final car and suggestions for decals and finishing.

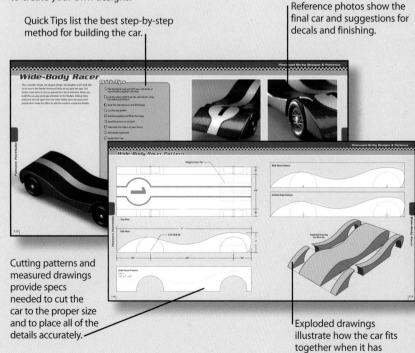

Cutting patterns and measured drawings provide specs needed to cut the car to the proper size and to place all of the details accurately.

Exploded drawings illustrate how the car fits together when it has multiple wood blocks.

Chapter 1
Getting Started

Start creating a Pinewood Derby car not by jumping right in and making the first cuts, but by understanding the tools you'll need, learning how to use them, and gathering the ones that best suit your working style. This is also the perfect time to go over safety procedures with your child so that he knows how to stay safe throughout the building process.

This chapter provides an overview of the most common woodworking tools and supplies needed to design and build your Pinewood Derby car safely and effectively. For each item, a brief description and suggested instructions for its use are provided, along with tips on which items work best for specific tasks. The information in this chapter will not only aid you in selecting tools and supplies, but also help you familiarize your child with the tools he'll be using.

Safety

Building a Pinewood Derby car with your child can be very rewarding, provided that you make safety a priority. As you prepare to make the car, keep the following safety points in mind.

- **Take stock of your workspace.** Make sure that it is clean and neat. Check for adequate lighting and ventilation.

- **Remember to supervise your child** as he uses any power tools. Remind him of any safety procedures—such as securing loose clothing, hair, or jewelry before he turns on any tool.

- **Always follow the manufacturer's instructions** on any items that you use.

Additionally, have the following safety items readily available and use them throughout the project to ensure a positive experience for you and your child.

Melting or Sanding Lead

Beware of any Pinewood Derby websites and "how to win" books and videos that recommend melting or sanding lead. These techniques are very dangerous and will not help you win the Derby. Remember, lead is very poisonous, and, when you melt it or sand it, you create lead dust and fumes that can easily be inhaled. Lead should only be handled by adults, and with appropriate safety precautions.

Gloves

For safety, wear rubber or latex gloves when working with glues, paints, and lead. If you don't wear gloves when working with lead, wash your hands thoroughly afterward. Leather gloves that fit snugly can be helpful when working with sharp tools.

Safety Glasses

Eye protection is very important when sanding wood and working with power tools. Invest in safety glasses or goggles that protect your eyes and your child's eyes from the front and the sides.

Dust Masks

Wear dust masks to protect against harmful fumes and airborne particles when sanding, applying graphite, and spray painting. Form the metal strip at the top of the mask over the bridge of your child's nose to create a tight seal.

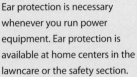

Ear Protection

Ear protection is necessary whenever you run power equipment. Ear protection is available at home centers in the lawncare or the safety section.

Be Trustworthy

As you gather the tools and materials for the building process, review the official and local Pinewood Derby rules and the Official Grand Prix Pinewood Derby car specifications. The list of suggested rules that accompanies each Official Grand Prix Pinewood Derby Kit® is shown at right and the specifications are illustrated below. If you don't have a copy of your local rules, ask your local race committee for one. Then abide by all of them. Remember, when you compete in the Pinewood Derby, be honest. If one of the designs in this book does not fit within your local Derby's rules, don't use it. If you are unsure whether something is legal, check with your local race organizer before you build the car.

Official Grand Prix Pinewood Derby Rules

1. Wheel bearings and bushings are prohibited.

2. The car shall not ride on springs.

3. Only official Cub Scout Grand Prix Pinewood Derby wheels and axles are permitted.

4. Only dry lubricant is permitted.

5. Details, such as steering wheel and driver, are permissible as long as these details do not exceed the maximum length, width, and weight specifications.

6. The car must be free-wheeling, with no starting devices.

7. Each car must pass inspection by the official inspection committee before it may compete. If, at registration, a car does not pass inspection, the owner will be informed of the reason for failure and will be given time within the official weigh-in time period to make the adjustment. After approval, cars will not be re-inspected unless the car is damaged in handling or in a race.

Source: Boy Scouts of America Official Grand Prix Pinewood Derby Kit.

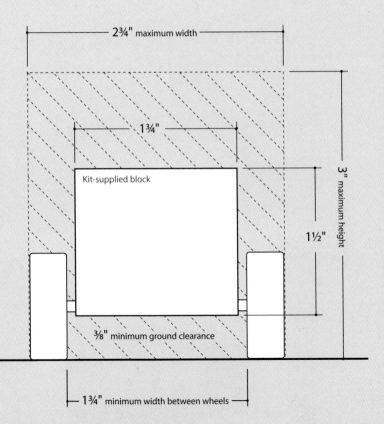

- 2¾" maximum width
- 1¾"
- Kit-supplied block
- 3" maximum height
- 1½"
- ⅜" minimum ground clearance
- 1¾" minimum width between wheels

Wood-Cutting Tools

Wood-cutting tools are essential for the initial, rough cuts that form the basis for your design.

The best and most efficient saws are the band saw, jigsaw, and scroll saw. However, these are not suitable for your child to use. If you have the time and would like to have your child cut the initial design, try letting him use a coping saw, with your guidance. This is a great way to get your child involved in the process.

Any time you use a cutting tool, install a sharp blade. Doing so will ensure safety and make cutting easier and less time-consuming for both you and your child. You don't want him to lose interest at this early stage.

Saw Safely

Saws are sharp and potentially dangerous tools if not used properly. Cut in a slow, deliberate manner. Do not force wood through the saw. Make sure your sawing area is clean. Eliminate distractions and keep your eyes on your work. Always wear safety glasses and a dust mask when working around wood-cutting tools.

Coping Saw

You can cut any of the patterns in this book with a coping saw. The main benefit of this saw is that children can easily use one. Take your time and check both sides of the car to ensure that the cuts are parallel to the block.

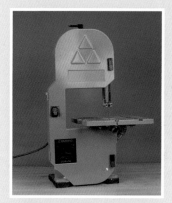

Band Saw

Small benchtop band saws are great for cutting out Pinewood Derby cars. A fine ⅛" blade produces the best results. Provide a secure platform that's a safe distance away from the front of the saw so your child can watch you cut and see how the saw works.

Jigsaw

If you choose to use a jigsaw, install a thin, fine wood blade to cut tighter curves, and use clamps to hold the block steady. You will need to reposition the clamps often.

Scroll Saw

Scroll saws are perfect for Pinewood Derby cars because their fine blades cut very tight curves; however, they can only cut wood less than 2½" thick. Remember to find a safe spot for your child to stand and watch.

Wood-Shaping Tools

After you cut the pattern out of the wooden block, you and your child must shape it into its final form. Below are wood-shaping tools and supplies that are recommended for shaping your Derby car. With your guidance, your child can easily and safely use all of these shaping tools. Allow him to participate in this process so that he feels involved in building the car. The fine wood dust these tools create is a health hazard, however, so be sure that both you and your child wear a dust mask and goggles.

Sandpaper

Use four different sandpaper grits, such as 100, 150, 220, and 400, for your car. Cut each sheet of sandpaper into four pieces. Then, fold one piece in half and then in half again. As the sandpaper wears out, refold the paper to expose a fresh area. This technique makes the paper last longer.

Small Files

Small files, available at home centers, rough shape wood and fillers. They can also remove the burrs on the axles supplied with the Pinewood Derby kit.

Power Sanders

Random orbit and pad sanders sand large areas. They can be used for flat or convex surfaces.

Sanding Sticks

Sand the car with homemade sanding sticks. To make these, simply glue sandpaper to one end of a craft stick with spray mount and then cut around the edge with scissors. Make four sticks (one grit per stick) using 100-, 150-, 220-, and 400-grit sandpaper. Use a marker to write the grit number on the back of the stick.

Profile Sanders

Profile sanders come with a wide range of rubber profiles. Special adhesive-backed sandpaper wraps around the profiles allowing the sander to sand hard-to-reach areas.

Wood-Cutting & Wood-Shaping Tools

Wood-Shaping Tools

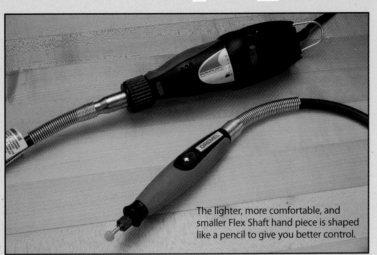

The lighter, more comfortable, and smaller Flex Shaft hand piece is shaped like a pencil to give you better control.

Shaping Tools

A Dremel® or similar tool is the most useful shaping tool for your Pinewood Derby car. It cuts quickly and accepts a wide range of bits. The speed, which ranges from 5,000 to 35,000 rpm, can be adjusted using the variable speed control. Slower speeds offer more control while faster speeds can remove material quickly. The optional Flex Shaft hand piece gives you better control.

After attaching the Flex Shaft to the Dremel tool, hang the motor (which is separate from the hand piece) on a hook above your workbench. This setup decreases vibration and prevents the motor from falling off the workbench and pulling the bit from your hand.

Bits

The basic bits that come with most shaping tools are also some of the most useful. The set often includes small, steel cylinder cutters and the large and small drum sanders. If you decide to purchase additional bits, choose the cylinder-shaped Structured Tooth Tungsten Carbide Cutter (9933). It has many uses, from shaping the outside of a car to cutting out the material inside a car.

Always wear safety glasses and a dust mask when using a shaping tool. Use hearing protection for your child; most children find the tool's high-pitched noise intolerable.

Whenever you cut with a bit for the first time, practice on a scrap piece of wood before trying it on your car. It takes a few minutes to gauge how the bit cuts best. The wood grain will cause the bit to cut cleaner in one direction than the other.

Useful Dremel Bits

Small High Speed Cutter (193)

Large High Speed Cutter (196)

Cylinder-shaped Structured Tooth Tungsten Carbide Cutter (9933)

Cone-shaped Structured Tooth Tungsten Carbide Cutter (9934)

¼" Sanding Drum (430)

½" Sanding Drum (407)

1¼" Cut-off Disk (426)

Dremel Chuck (4486)

Supplies

Generally, Derby cars don't require a lot of different supplies. Many are common household items. These items can also be purchased from your local home center.

Work in a Well-Ventilated Area

When using wood filler, glue, and other adhesives, be sure to follow the manufacturer's instructions. Work in a well-ventilated area. Be sure lids are closed tightly before storing. Avoid contact with eyes and skin by wearing protective gloves and goggles.

Solder

Solder works well for making detailed parts for your Derby car. Purchase lead-free silver solder. It bends easily by hand but is strong enough to survive being handled by children. It can be used to make exhaust pipes, roll bars, and bumpers.

Adhesives

Spray mount, epoxy, cyanoacrylate glue (CA glue), and wood glue are all important for building a Derby car. Use spray mount to attach patterns to blocks of wood. Epoxy is a very strong bonding glue used to attach wood and metal parts together. CA glue is fast drying and can quickly glue small wooden parts together—or your fingers together if you aren't careful. Wood glue is best for gluing large pieces of wood together.

Tape

Blue painter's tape is the best all-around tape. It has many uses—from taping off areas before painting to holding wood together during the sawing process. Blue ⅛" fine-line tape makes perfect paint lines. Pinstriping tape is a great way to hide an imperfect paint edge.

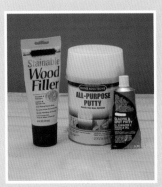

Wood Fillers

Because all of the cars in this book are painted, don't choose the standard wood-matching fillers. They are slow drying and brittle. Instead, use fast-drying fillers.

Copper Wire and Soldering Iron

To construct detailed items, such as steering wheels, suspension parts, and window frames, use copper ground wire. This 14-gauge electrical wire is easy to solder with a simple soldering iron.

Paint Supplies

A perfect paint job isn't as hard to achieve as you might think. It's all about planning, preparing, and having patience. Always remember to wear a dust mask and to paint in a well-ventilated area.

Acrylic craft paints are great for kids to use because they clean up easily with soap and water. Most craft stores carry a wide variety of colors, and these paints cost only about one dollar per bottle.

Small Testors® enamel paints are available in many flat and gloss colors. They can be brushed on or thinned and sprayed through an airbrush. You can purchase enamel paints at most home centers.

Spray paint primers are available in white, gray, and red. Primer is the base coat applied before the color coat. It dries fast and sands better than regular spray paint.

Spray paint comes in a wide variety of colors. Always use the same brand of primer, color coat, and clear coat throughout the project. Otherwise, your paint may not set properly.

Spray clear coat adds a shiny finish. It can also protect pinstripes and decals from wear.

Automotive-quality spray paint can create a finish that looks as if it came from an auto body shop. Some brands come in a three-step process, such as candy base coat, color coat, and clear coat. These paint systems are available in candy and pearl finishes.

Weights

You can use different types of weight for your Pinewood Derby car, including lead, tungsten, and zinc. Lead works best because of its high weight-to-mass ratio, its availability, and its variety of sizes and shapes. Fishing sinkers are a good source of lead and are available in many different sizes. Split shot and egg-shaped sinkers are the best kinds of sinkers to use in Pinewood Derby cars. Remember to use safety measures when working with lead (see "Safety" on page 2).

Lead wire is also available. Most often, it is inserted into $^{25}/_{64}$" drilled holes. It is easier to use than split shot but harder to find. Purchase lead wire from online retailers.

Like lead, tungsten is another excellent choice with a high weight-to-mass ratio. Unfortunately, tungsten can be expensive and hard to find.

Zinc has a lower density than lead and tungsten. Therefore, you must use more zinc than you would if you used lead or tungsten. For this reason, I would not recommend zinc for Derby cars.

Be Cautious with Lead

Always remember that lead is a toxic substance. Keep all lead products out of the reach of young children, and follow all warnings that accompany lead products. If you add lead weights to your Derby car, either wear gloves when handling the lead or wash your hands thoroughly when you're finished handling it. And never use melted lead! Melting lead is a dangerous activity, and there is no reason to use this technique. You can safely add weight to your car using other forms of lead. Lead should only be handled by adults, and with appropriate safety precautions.

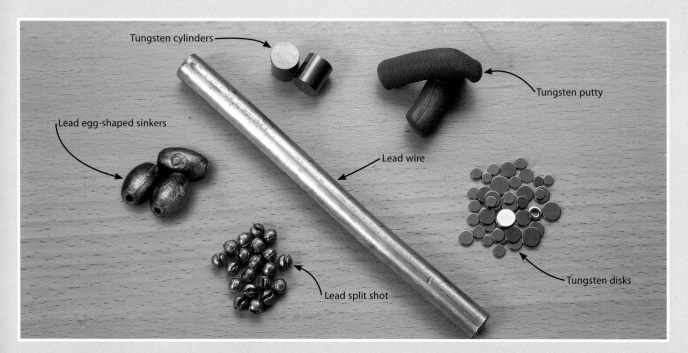

Tungsten cylinders

Tungsten putty

Lead egg-shaped sinkers

Lead wire

Tungsten disks

Lead split shot

Adding Weight

After you finish shaping and before you paint your car, you need to add weight to get the car close to the maximum 5.0 ounces. I recommend adding weight up to 4.8 ounces, which leaves 0.2 ounces for paint and decals. Though there are various weights you can use (see "Weights" on page 9), egg-shaped lead sinkers work best for the designs in this book. Remember to follow all safety measures when working with lead (see "Safety" on page 2).

Place the weight in the rear of your car to get the maximum speed benefit; however, do not place the weight completely behind the rear axle. Centering all of the weight behind the rear axle will make the front end of your car too light, and the car will not run straight down the track. Or, in the worst-case scenario, the car might jump off the track. The instructions below show you a simple way to add weight to the designs in this book.

Materials and Tools

- Small digital scale
- Six ¼-oz. egg-shaped lead sinkers
- Latex gloves
- Pencil
- File
- Hammer
- Safety glasses
- Dust mask

- Dremel or other shaping tool and bit:
  - Cylinder-shaped Structured Tooth Tungsten Carbide Cutter (9933)
- Wood filler, such as Bondo
- 220-grit sandpaper
- Soft cloth

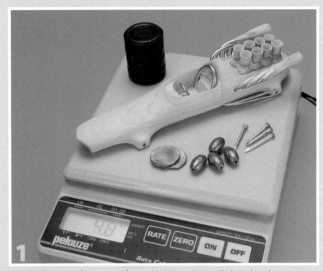

Weigh all parts of your car. If you don't have a small digital scale, you can take the car to your local post office and ask them to weigh the car. Add ¼-ounce egg-shaped lead sinkers until the weight is about 4.8 ounces.

To fit the lead in the smallest cavity in the car, pound the egg-shaped sinkers into flat disks about ⅛" thick, using a hammer. This car, the Vintage Racecar from page 40, requires six ¼-ounce egg-shaped lead sinkers.

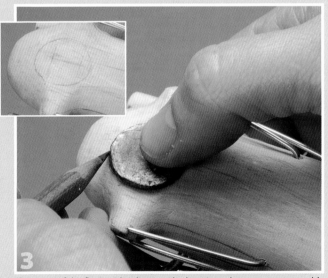

Place one of the flattened sinkers on the location where you want to add the weight. Trace around the sinker with a pencil. Remember to wash your hands thoroughly after handling lead or wear latex gloves.

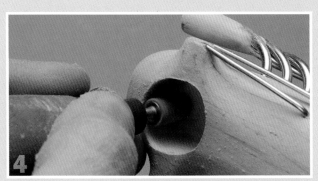

Use a shaping tool with a cylinder-shaped tungsten carbide cutter to cut a hole in the car.

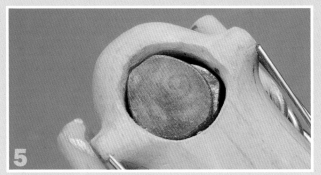

Stack the lead pieces in the hole. The top piece should be about 1/16" below the surface of the car.

Mix a small amount of wood filler. Press the filler into the hole and use it to cover the lead completely. Then, set the car aside and allow the filler to dry according to the manufacturer's directions.

Once the filler has dried, sand it flush with the car. Start with a file and then use 220-grit sandpaper.

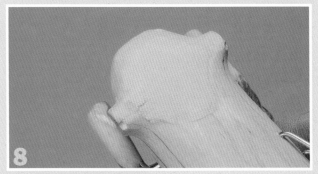

Wipe off any dust with a soft cloth.

Oops . . . Fixing a Mistake

When you mix up a batch of wood filler, take a few minutes to fill in any unwanted dents or dings left in the wood.

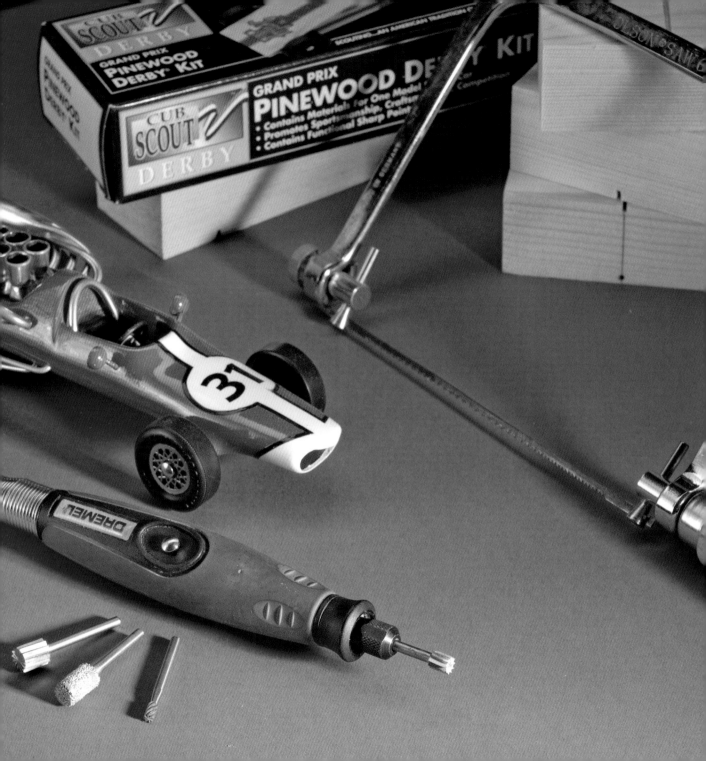

Chapter 2
Building the Cars

  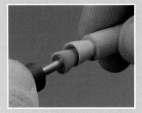 

Building the car body and its accessories sets the stage for turning your car into something special. This chapter features three different designs—the High-Wing Racer, the Stock Car, and the Vintage Racecar. The process for each car is demonstrated through step-by-step instructions and corresponds to a particular skill level: beginning, intermediate, and advanced. The simple High-Wing Racer uses the standard slots and wheelbase. The more-advanced Stock Car features a realistic-looking design, created by adding wood to the official Pinewood Derby block. The Vintage Racecar is the no-holds-barred design challenge. Whichever design you choose, work as a team to get the best results. Remember to make the building process fun and encourage your child to stretch his imagination as you build a car together.

High-Wing Racer

This high-wing racecar jumps right out of the history books—back when bigger was better. This project uses only the wood supplied in the official BSA® kit. It's also designed to use the standard wheelbase and kit-supplied axle slots. With a simple shape, some easy sanding, a one-color paint job, and some creative decaling, you will have a car that both you and your child can be proud of.

Materials and Tools

- Copies of Cutting Pattern, page 17
- Copies of window patterns, taken from Cutting Pattern, page 17
- Official Grand Prix Pinewood Derby Kit
- Pencil
- Ruler
- Scissors
- Coping saw, scroll saw, band saw, or jigsaw
- Dust mask

- Dremel or other shaping tool and bit:
  - Cylinder-shaped Structured Tooth Tungsten Carbide Cutter (9933)
- Low-tack spray mount
- Cyanoacrylate (CA) glue
- Craft sticks
- Several sheets each of 120- and 220-grit sandpaper
- Weights of choice
- Safety glasses
- Gloves

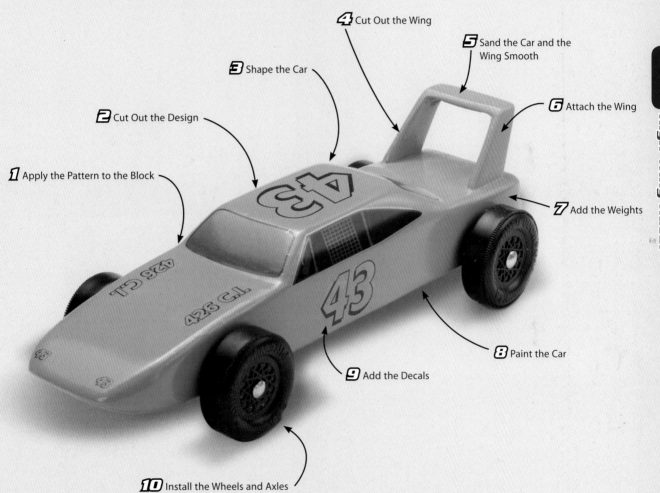

4 Cut Out the Wing

5 Sand the Car and the Wing Smooth

3 Shape the Car

6 Attach the Wing

2 Cut Out the Design

1 Apply the Pattern to the Block

7 Add the Weights

8 Paint the Car

9 Add the Decals

10 Install the Wheels and Axles

Measured Drawings

Top View

7"

1¼

Side View

15⁄16 "

Wing

¾"

Cutting Pattern

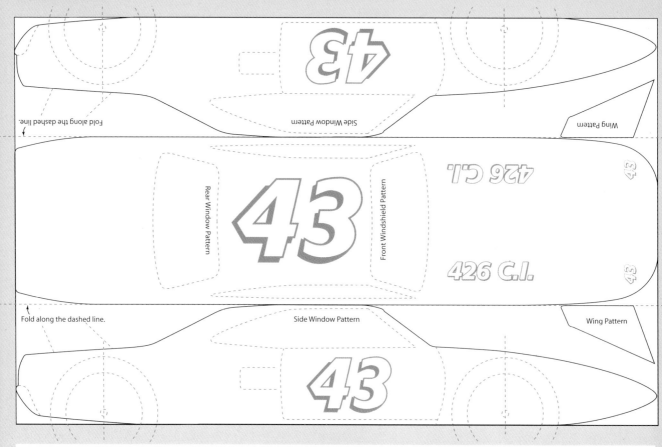

Fold along the dashed line.

Side Window Pattern

Wing Pattern

Rear Window Pattern

Front Windshield Pattern

426 C.I.

426 C.I.

Fold along the dashed line.

Side Window Pattern

Wing Pattern

Decal Art

You can scan the artwork here and print them on special transfer paper to create custom decals for your car. See the demonstration on page 72 for more information adding decals to your car.

Side Windows

Front Windshield

Rear Window

Door Numbers

Roof Number

Hood Numbers

Hood Decals

Taillights

1 Make a few copies of the Cutting Pattern on page 17.

2 Trim around the outside of the pattern with scissors, cutting exactly on the outside pattern lines. Then, fold the pattern along the dashed lines.

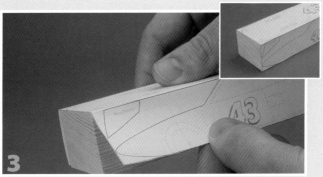

3 Lightly spray the back of the pattern with spray mount. (Be sure to spray the pattern and not the wood.) Wrap the pattern around the sides and top of the block supplied in the Pinewood Derby kit.

4 Cut out the car body with a scroll saw or the saw of your choice, using the side profile of the Cutting Pattern.

5 Next, cut the Wing Pattern from the side profile.

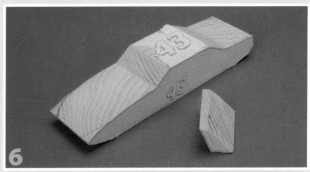

6 Using the top of the Cutting Pattern as reference, draw the rounded corners on the front and back of the car with a pencil. Then, remove the paper patterns.

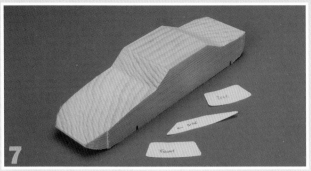

7 Use the saw to cut off the rounded corners. Then, using scissors, cut out the window patterns, taken from the Cutting Pattern on page 17.

8 Draw a centerline down the top of the car. Fold the Front Windshield Pattern in half to find the center. Line up the centerlines of the car and the front windshield, and trace the windshield shape onto the car.

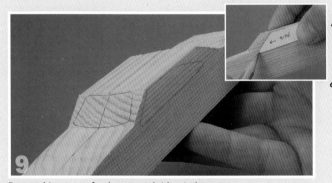

9 Repeat this process for the rear and side windows.

Don't Have a Scroll Saw?

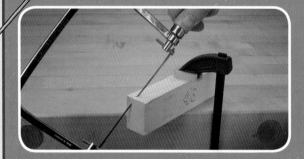

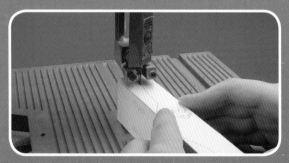

If you don't have access to a scroll saw, try using a coping saw, a jigsaw, or even a band saw. Pine is a soft wood that can be easily cut with any saw.

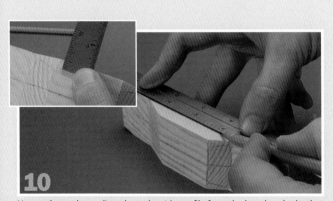

10 Use a ruler to draw a line along the side profile from the hood to the back trunk deck of the car. The line should be even with the bottom of the side window. Then, on the roof of the car, draw a line ¼" in from each side.

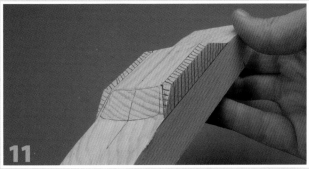

11 Connect the lines along the window pillars in the front and back, as shown in the photo. The shaded material will be removed.

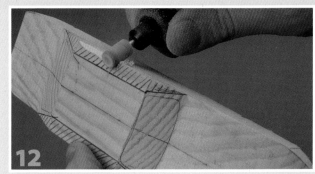

12 Using a cylinder-shaped tungsten carbide cutter mounted in a shaping tool, cut away the material in the shaded area.

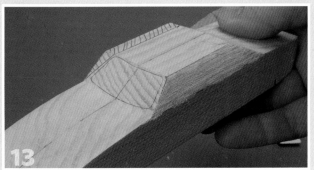

13 Remove the material up to the roof line. Repeat this process for the other side.

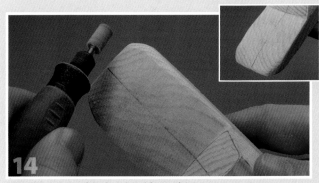

14 Round the edges of the hood and front of the car.

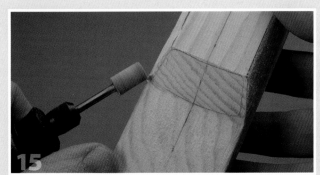

15 The next step is to create the curve of the front windshield. First, cut a curved groove into the base of the windshield on the outside right corner. Make sure that you don't cut into the hood of the car. Do this on both sides.

16 Mark the material you'll remove from the outside edge of the left side of the windshield, as shown in the photo. The step will continue to create the curve of the windshield. The straight reference line will help you see how the curve is beginning to take shape.

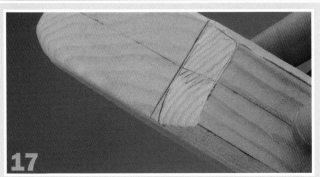

This is how the windshield should look after you remove the material on the left side.

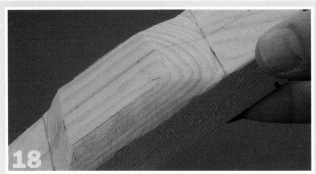

Repeat the same process on the right side of the windshield and on the back window.

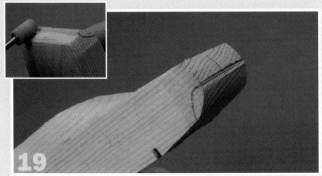

Use the Cutting Pattern as a reference to draw the rear bumper on the car. Use the shaping tool with the tungsten carbide cutter to remove some material from the back of the trunk. The bumper should stick out approximately 1/16" from the trunk.

Use the shaping tool with the tungsten carbide cutter to round the trunk and the roof edges.

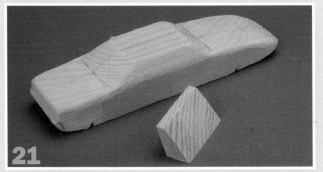

Look over the car body and make any final adjustments if desired. Now we're ready to cut the rear wing to shape.

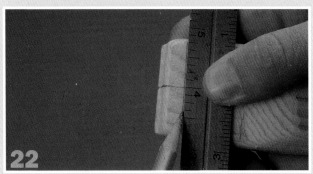

On the trunk of the car, draw a line 1/4" in from the back. The back of the wing will sit on this line.

23

Hold the wing on the car. Mark ⅛" in from both sides of the car to set the width of the wing. Then, extend the lines to the top of the wing. The dashed lines are reference lines. At the top of the wing, place a second mark that is ⅛" in from both reference lines. Draw lines that connect the second marks and the ends of the first lines—these create the wing taper and will be your cut lines.

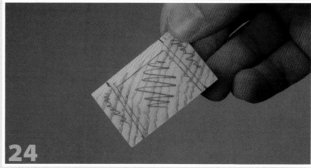

24

Transfer the cut lines to the front of the wing. Measure ⅛" in from these lines along the sides and top of the wing to form the inside edges.

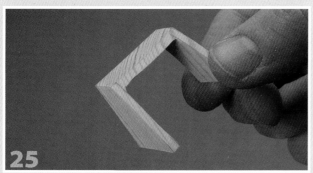

25

Carefully cut the wing with the saw of your choice. Remove the inside of the wing first and then cut along the outside.

26

Sand the car with 120-grit sandpaper that has been spray mounted to a craft stick. Sand until the car is smooth. Then, hand sand the car with a folded piece of 220-grit sandpaper to remove the rough sandpaper marks.

Oops . . . Fixing a Broken Wing

If the wing breaks while you're cutting it out, simply add a little CA glue to the broken area, and hold the broken parts together for a few minutes until the glue dries. Then, continue cutting out the wing.

27

Sand the wing with the sanding stick and then with the 220-grit sandpaper. Be careful not to crack the wing at the top.

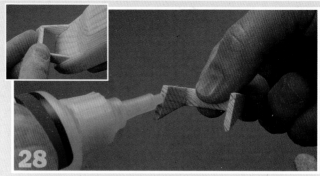

28

Use CA glue to attach the wing to the car. Hold the wing in place for a few minutes to allow the glue to set.

29

Here is the finished car before painting. Add weight to the car before you paint it (see "Adding Weight" on page 10).

Stock Car

Though stock car racing is considered a U.S.-centered pastime, interest in the sport is growing around the world. For this project, I've supplied artwork for making your own Cub Scout–sponsored stock car, complete with your pack number as the car number. Or, if you prefer, you can build a Pinewood Derby car to match your favorite driver's. Sheets of plastic scale-model decals are available from online retailers. The 1:24 scale models are close to the size of this stock car pattern.

This project requires a little more work than the High-Wing Racer on page 14. You will need three blocks of wood to build this car, in addition to what is supplied in the BSA kit. Your local home center will have wood available in the thicknesses listed below and may even be able to cut wood to the size you want. Check your local rules and read the maximum size allowed before completing this car. This pattern is smaller than the maximum size listed on the official BSA rules that accompany the kit.

Materials and Tools

- Copies of Wheel Well Cutting Pattern, page 27
- Copies of Axle-Drilling Pattern, page 26
- Copies of Cutting Pattern, page 26
- Copies of Hood, Grill, Front Windshield, and Rear Window Patterns, page 26
- Copies of Side Window Patterns, page 26
- Copies of Rear Pattern, page 27
- Official Grand Prix Pinewood Derby Kit
- Extra wood:
  - 2 side blocks, 7" x 1¾" x ½" each
  - Top block, 7" x 1¾" x ¼"

- Pencil
- Black marker
- Ruler
- Scissors
- Utility knife
- Coping saw, scroll saw, band saw, or jigsaw
- Dremel or shaping tool and bits:
  - ½" 60-grit Sanding Drum (407)
  - Small High Speed Cutter (194)
- Drill press or Derby Worx axle-drilling jig and power drill
- #44 drill bit
- Speed clamps

- 3 T-pins or small nails
- Three ½"-long brad nails
- 1"-wide painter's tape
- Low-tack spray mount
- Wood glue
- Several sheets each of 120- and 220-grit sandpaper
- Craft sticks
- ⅜" dowel
- Damp rag
- Empty aluminum soda can
- Weights of choice
- Safety glasses
- Dust mask
- Gloves

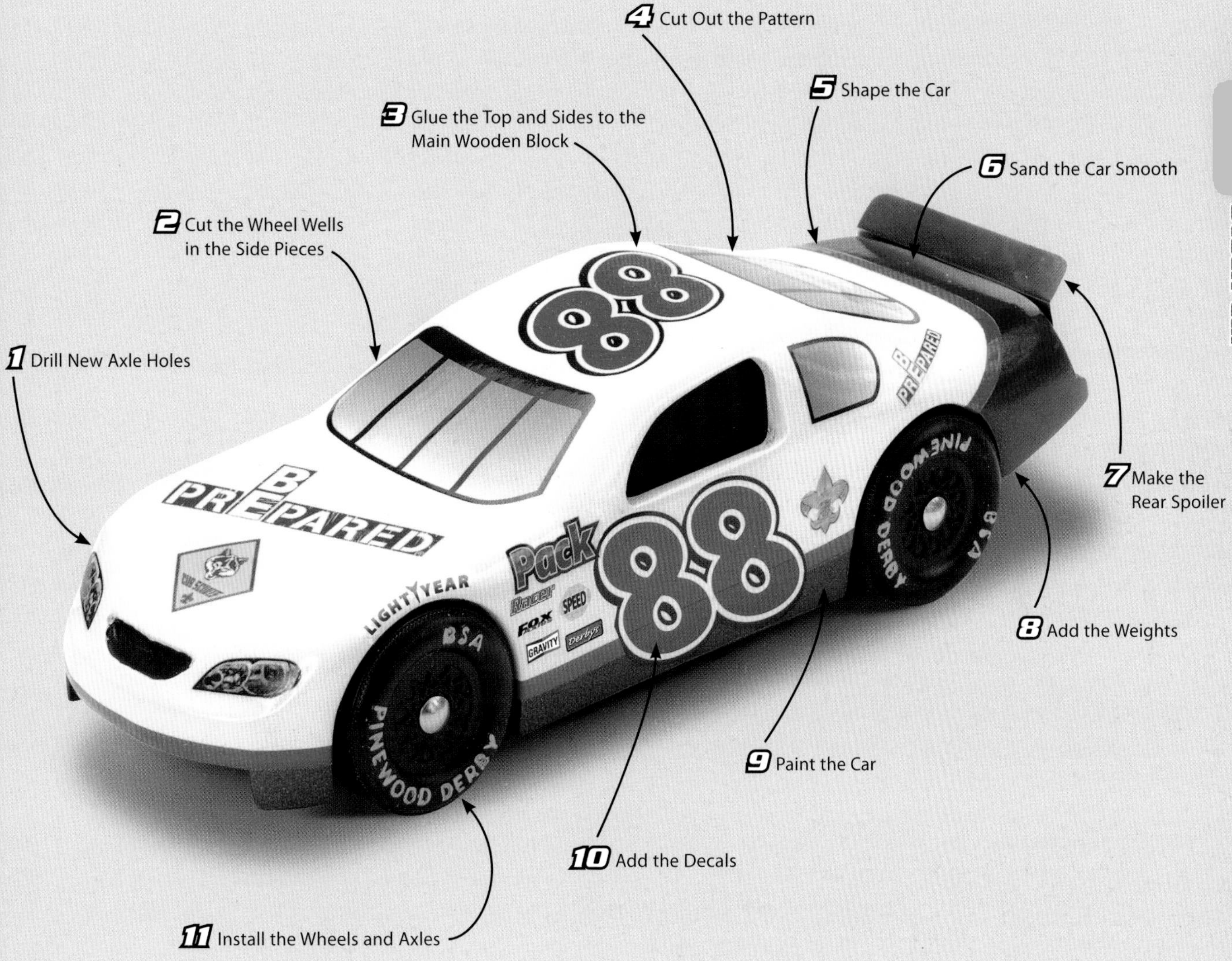

4 Cut Out the Pattern

5 Shape the Car

3 Glue the Top and Sides to the Main Wooden Block

6 Sand the Car Smooth

2 Cut the Wheel Wells in the Side Pieces

1 Drill New Axle Holes

7 Make the Rear Spoiler

8 Add the Weights

9 Paint the Car

10 Add the Decals

11 Install the Wheels and Axles

Stock Car Pattern

Cutting Pattern

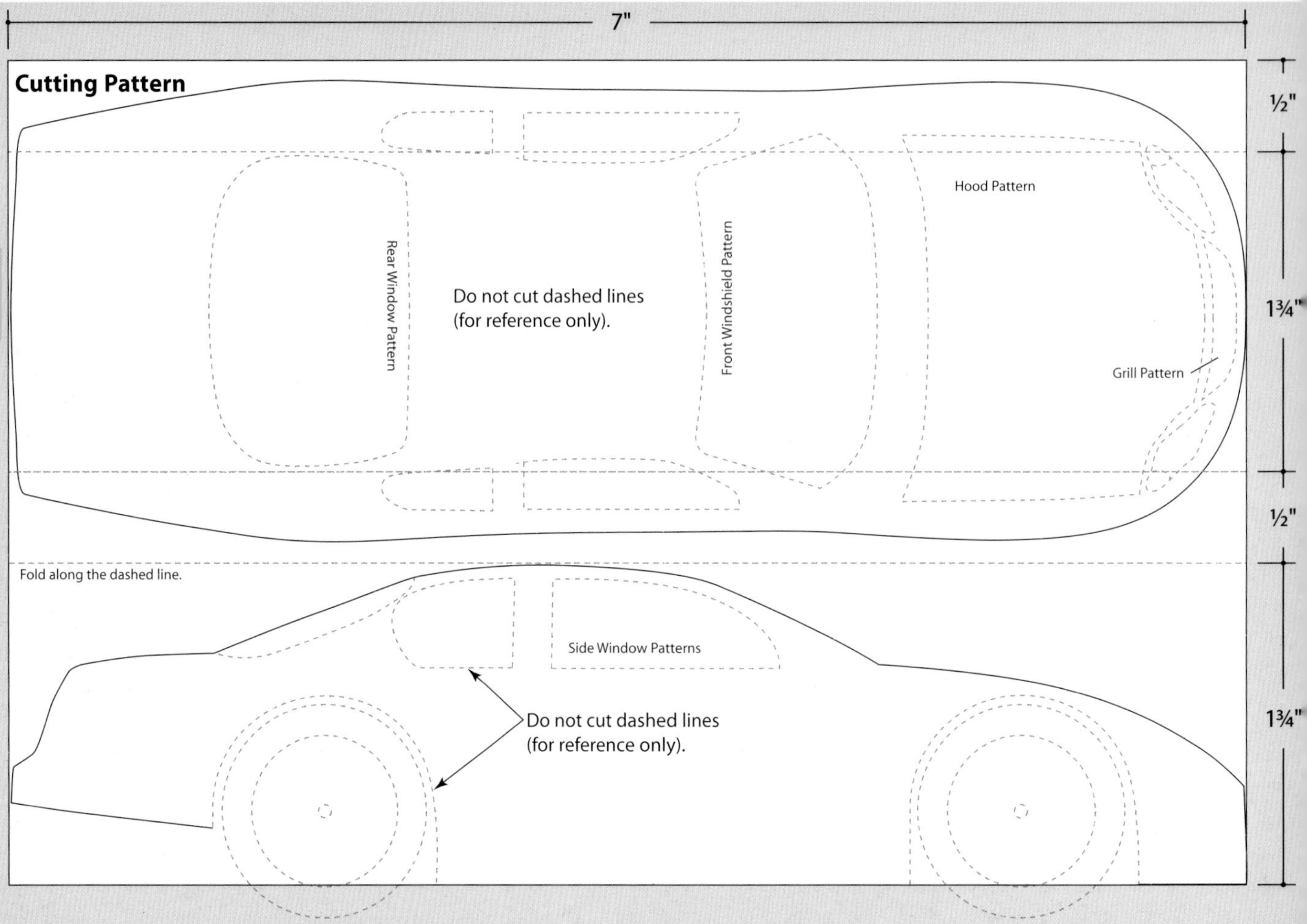
7"
Rear Window Pattern
Do not cut dashed lines
(for reference only).
Front Windshield Pattern
Hood Pattern
Grill Pattern
Fold along the dashed line.
Side Window Patterns
Do not cut dashed lines
(for reference only).
½"
1¾"
½"
1¾"

Axle-Drilling Pattern

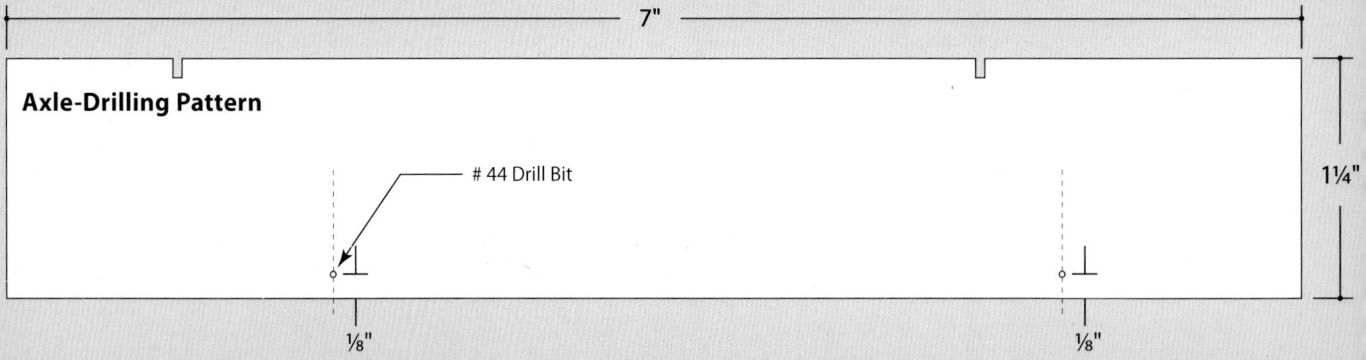
7"
44 Drill Bit
1¼"
⅛"
⅛"

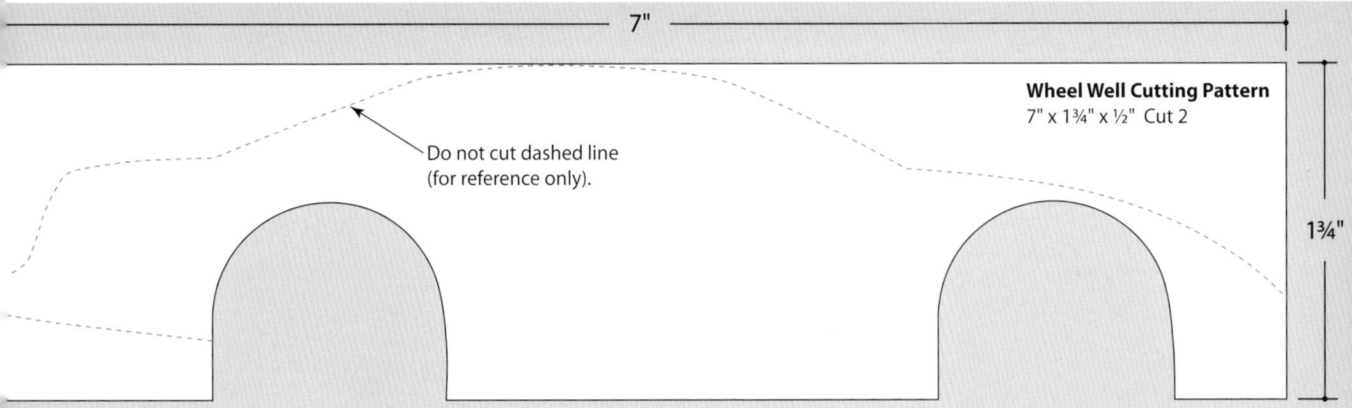

Wheel Well Cutting Pattern
7" x 1¾" x ½" Cut 2

7"

1¾"

Do not cut dashed line
(for reference only).

Rear Pattern

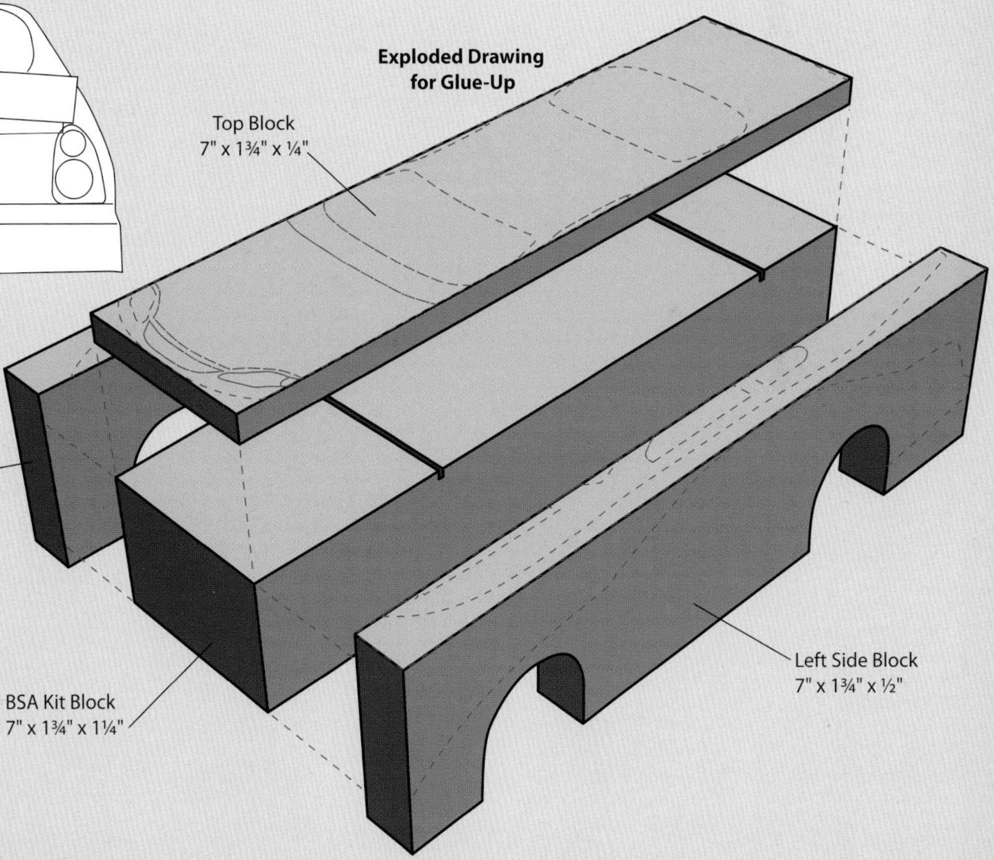

**Exploded Drawing
for Glue-Up**

Top Block
7" x 1¾" x ¼"

Right Side Block
7" x 1¾" x ½"

BSA Kit Block
7" x 1¾" x 1¼"

Left Side Block
7" x 1¾" x ½"

You can scan the artwork on these pages and print them on special transfer paper to create custom decals for your car. See the demonstration on page 72 for more information on adding decals to your car.

Rear Trunk Designs

Rear Fender Designs

Hood Designs

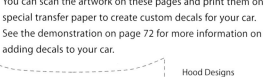

B PREPARED

B PREPARED

Rear Trunk Designs

Rear Fender Designs

Pack 88

Pack 88

28

Passenger Side Sponsors

Front Fender
Sponsors

Driver Side Sponsors

Roof Numbers

12345 67890

Taillights

Headlights

Front Windshield

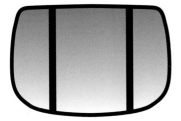

Rear Side
Windows

Rear Window

Driver Side
Door Numbers

12345 67890

Passenger Side
Door Numbers

12345 67890

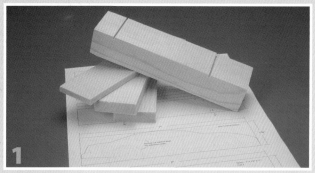

1. Gather your materials. Start with the kit block, the two side blocks, the top block, and a few copies of the patterns on pages 26 and 27. See the Materials and Tools list on page 24 for the sizes of the side and top blocks.

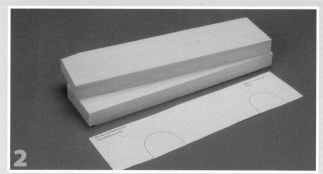

2. Cut out the Wheel Well Cutting Pattern from page 27 with scissors.

3. Stack the two side blocks together and wrap 1"-wide painter's tape around the outer edges.

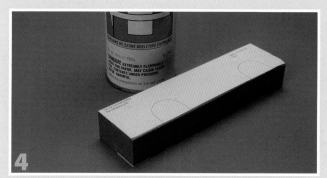

4. Lightly apply spray mount to the bottom of the Wheel Well Cutting Pattern and attach the pattern to the top of the side blocks.

5. Use a scroll saw or the saw of your choice to cut out the wheel wells.

6. Remove the front and back wheel wells. Then, remove the pattern and tape.

Use a shaping tool with a ½" 60-grit sanding drum attachment to sand the wheel wells.

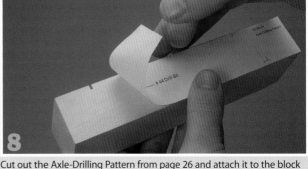

Cut out the Axle-Drilling Pattern from page 26 and attach it to the block supplied in the BSA kit. Flip the block over so that the BSA axle slots will be on the top of the block.

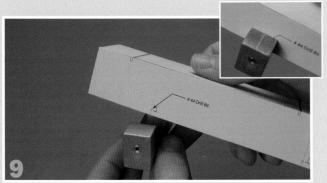

Measure and drill the holes with a drill press or use a Derby Worx axle-drilling jig. Line up the center mark on the jig with the axle hole centerline on the pattern.

Clamp the block if necessary with wood clamps and drill the holes with a #44 drill bit.

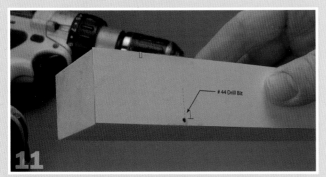

Remove the pattern once you have drilled all four axle holes.

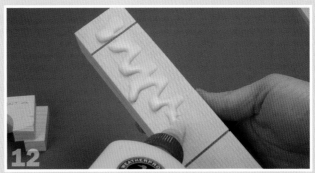

Apply wood glue to the top of the kit block and the bottom of the top block, making sure that you have a thin coat on both surfaces.

13 Spread out the glue evenly. It's important to have even coverage because you will be removing part of the block later on, and the block could come apart if the glue is not evenly distributed.

14 Clamp the top block to the kit block. Allow the glue to dry.

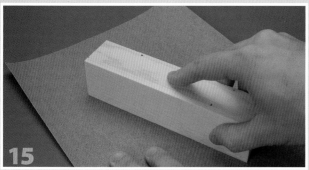

15 Place a sheet of 120-grit sandpaper on a flat surface. Sand the sides of the block until the glue joint is smooth.

16 Use the same process shown in Steps 12 through 15 to glue on the side block. Make sure the axle holes are centered in the wheel wells. Use a damp rag to remove any glue in the wheel wells.

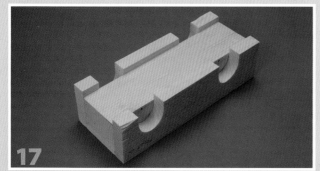

17 Repeat the process for the second side block. The recessed area on the bottom of the car will ride over the guide rail on the Pinewood Derby track.

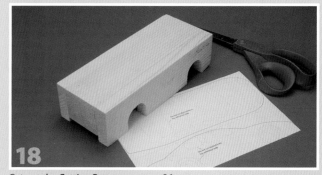

18 Cut out the Cutting Pattern on page 26.

19

Fold the pattern along the dashed line and apply a light coating of spray mount to the pattern. Attach the pattern to the block.

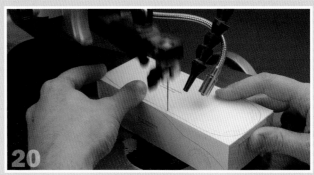

20

Cut along the top profile of the pattern using a scroll saw or the saw of your choice.

21

Be sure to cut off the scrap pieces entirely, but do not discard them.

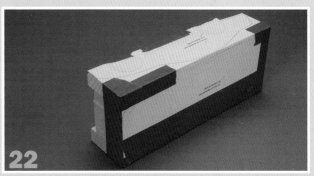

22

Reattach the side scrap pieces with painter's tape. Be careful not to cover the side profile of the pattern.

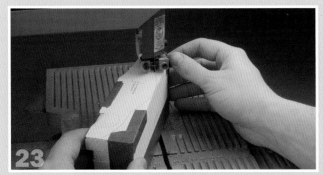

23

Use a band saw or a coping saw to trim along the side profile.

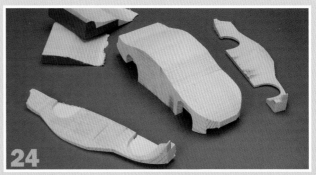

24

Remove all of the scrap pieces and patterns from the main block.

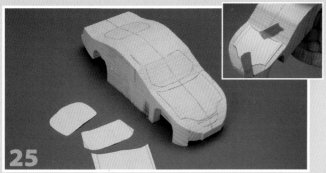

25

Trim out the Hood, Grill, Front Windshield, and Rear Window Patterns on page 26. Draw a centerline down the top of the car. Using the top profile of the Cutting Pattern on page 26 as location reference, hold the patterns in place with painter's tape and trace around them with a pencil.

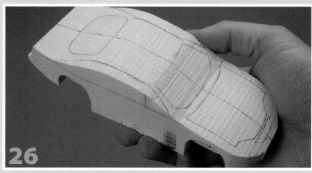

26

Draw a line along the side panel from the edge of the hood to the back trunk deck. Then, draw a line along the roof edge ¼" in from each side. Connect the lines to form the window pillars.

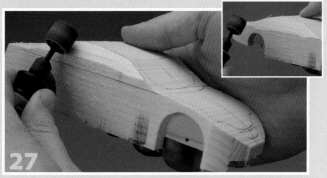

27

Using the shaping tool with the ½" 60-grit sanding drum, remove the material up to the reference lines. Removing this material creates the angled side window area and narrows the roof.

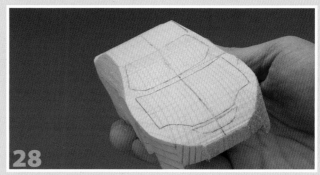

28

Remove the material from both sides. This is what your car should look like at this point.

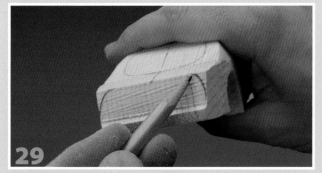

29

The next step is to round the rear deck, or trunk. Use the Rear Pattern on page 27 to create reference marks.

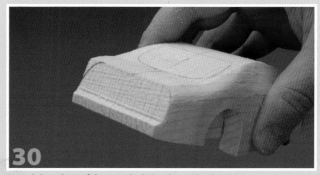

30

Round the edges of the rear deck. Do this on both sides.

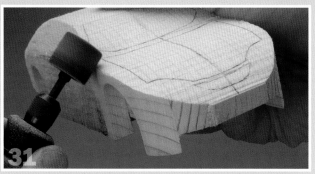

Round the edges of the front fender. Start at the rear of the hood and blend the side of the car into the top of the fender.

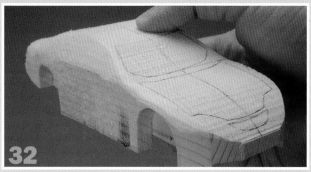

Continue rounding the front fender, but be careful not to round past the edge of the hood. Round both sides.

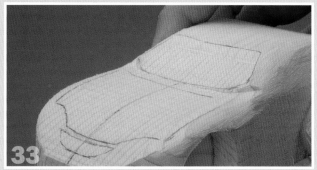

The next step is to curve the windshield. Cut a curved groove along the bottom edge of the front windshield outline using the drum sander. The groove should be even with the hood.

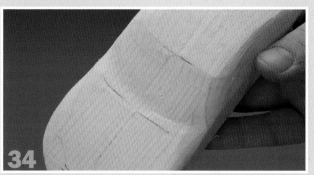

Carefully remove the material from the side edges of the windshield. Curve the windshield around to the side windows. Repeat this process for the back window.

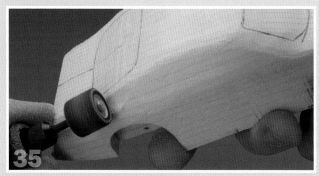

Round the area above the rear wheel wells.

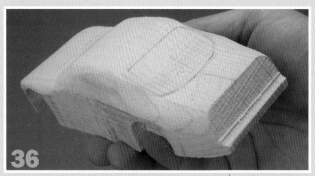

Create a smooth transition between the side windows and the rear deck.

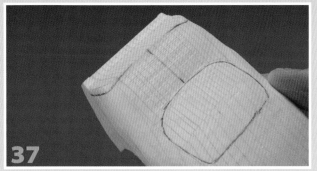

37

Draw the curvature of the rear trunk. Use the Cutting Pattern as reference.

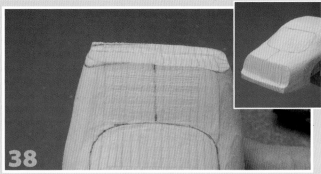

38

Remove the material with the shaping tool and the drum sander attachment.

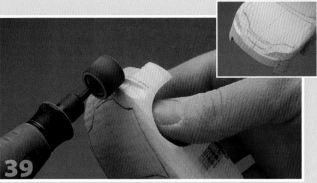

39

To create the headlight recesses, cut a ⅛"-deep groove above the front bumper on both sides. Use the Cutting Pattern as reference.

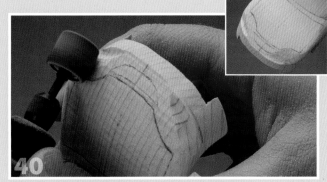

40

Round the area from the groove to the front of the hood.

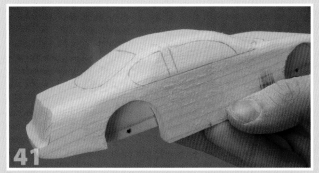

41

Cut out the Side Window Patterns on page 26 and draw them in place.

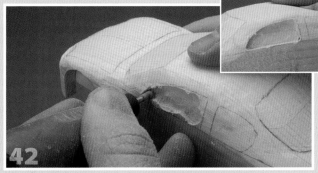

42

Using the shaping tool with a small high speed cutter, carefully cut a ³⁄₁₆"-deep recess in both front windows.

43 Redraw the front grill if necessary.

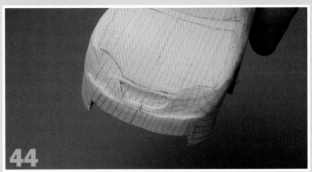

44 Use the small high speed cutter to remove approximately 1/16" of material from inside the grill opening.

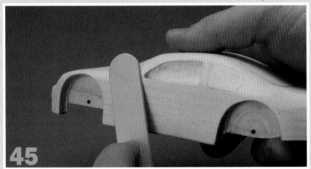

45 Use 120-grit sandpaper that has been spray mounted to a craft stick to block sand the car. Using a hard stick for this step will flatten any high spots.

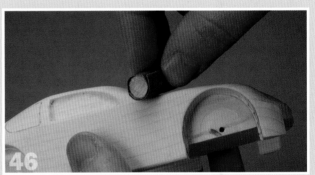

46 Wrap 120-grit sandpaper around a 3/8" dowel to sand the concave areas. Hand sand the car with 220-grit sandpaper to remove any deep scratches.

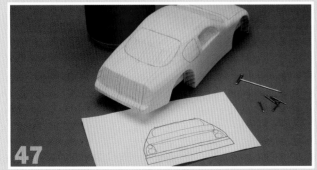

47 To make the spoiler, use the Rear Pattern on page 27 for reference. Choose a piece of thin aluminum for the spoiler—an empty aluminum soda can is the perfect material. Rinse out the soda can.

48 Have your child watch as you cut the soda can around the top and bottom edges with scissors. Dry the aluminum if needed. Be very careful with the sharp edges.

49

Cut a piece of aluminum about 3" x 1½" in size. Draw three straight lines ¼" apart with a black marker, such as a Sharpie.

50

Trim the aluminum along the outer two edges with scissors.

51

Place a ruler along the centerline and lightly score the aluminum with a utility knife.

52

Then, slowly bend the aluminum at the scoring line.

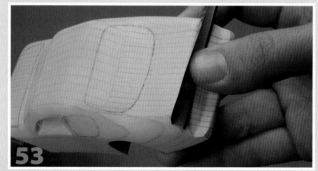

53

Hold the spoiler to the back of the car and mark it for width with the marker.

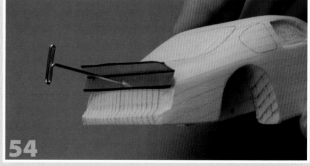

54

Use a T-pin or small nail in the center of the spoiler to hold it in place. Measure ⅝" in both directions from the pin and place two more T-pins.

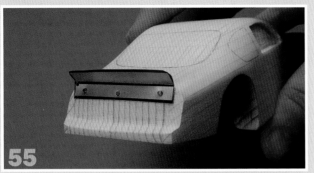

55

Remove the pins and spoiler so that you can easily round the corners of the spoiler. Remove any sharp edges with 220-grit sandpaper. Permanently hold the spoiler in place with three ½"-long brad nails after the car is painted. (The spoiler is shown installed temporarily on the unpainted car for reference.)

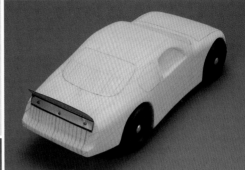

This is how the completed car should look before painting. (The wheels and the spoiler have been temporarily installed.) Add weight to the car before painting (see "Adding Weight" on page 10 for more details).

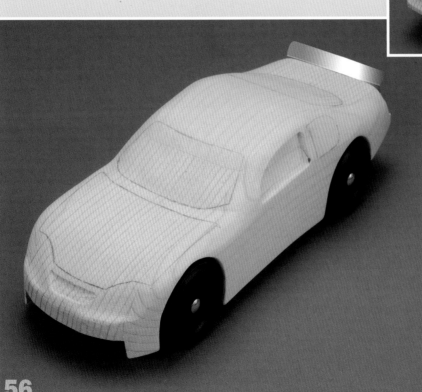

56

Vintage Racecar

Racecars from the 1950s and 1960s make great Pinewood Derby cars. Because of the open wheel design, their proportions are very close to the dimensions of the Pinewood Derby kit. Additionally, the open cockpits, exposed engines, and curvy exhaust pipes all provide added style. Although this design requires more time and steps, with patience, you and your child can work together to build an incredible Pinewood Derby car.

Materials and Tools

- Copies of Cutting Pattern, page 43
- Engine Patterns, page 43
- Official Grand Prix Pinewood Derby Kit
- Extra wood:
  - Intake manifold, 1½" x ¾" x ³⁄₁₆"
- Pencil
- Black marker
- Ruler
- Square
- Circle template
- Scissors
- Coping saw, scroll saw, band saw, or jigsaw
- Safety glasses
- Dust mask

- Dremel or shaping tool and bits:
  - Small High Speed Cutter (194)
  - Large High Speed Cutter (196)
  - Cylinder-shaped Structured Tooth Tungsten Carbide Cutter (9933)
  - Cone-shaped Structured Tooth Tungsten Carbide Cutter (9934)
  - 1¼" Cut-off Wheel (426)
  - ½" 60-grit Sanding Drum (407)
- Drill press or Derby Worx axle-drilling jig
- Power drill
- #44, ¹⁄₁₆", and ⅛" drill bits
- Speed clamps
- Bench vise
- Small flat file

- Small round file
- 40w soldering iron
- Electrical solder
- Lead-free plumbing repair solder
- Wire cutters
- 14-gauge electrical ground wire (available at most home centers)
- Low-tack spray mount
- 1"-wide painter's tape
- Cyanoacrylate (CA) glue
- 5-minute epoxy
- Wood filler, such as Bondo
- 120- and 220-grit sandpaper
- Craft sticks
- ⅜" dowels
- Weights of choice

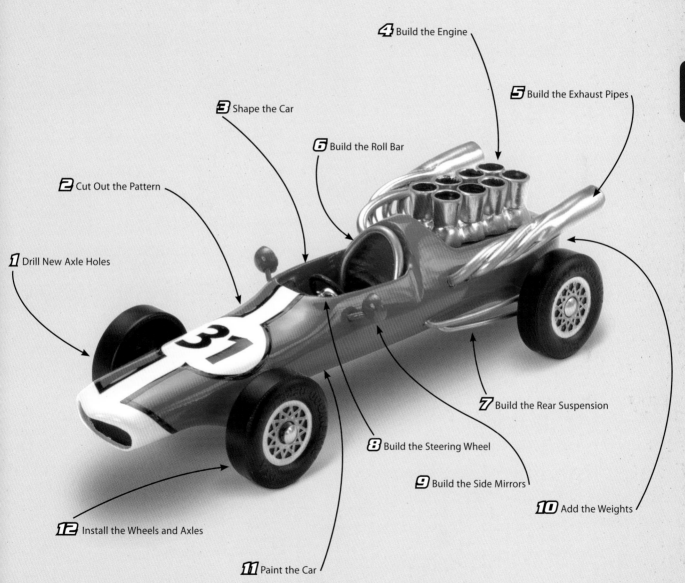

4 Build the Engine

5 Build the Exhaust Pipes

3 Shape the Car

6 Build the Roll Bar

2 Cut Out the Pattern

1 Drill New Axle Holes

7 Build the Rear Suspension

8 Build the Steering Wheel

9 Build the Side Mirrors

10 Add the Weights

12 Install the Wheels and Axles

11 Paint the Car

Measured Drawings

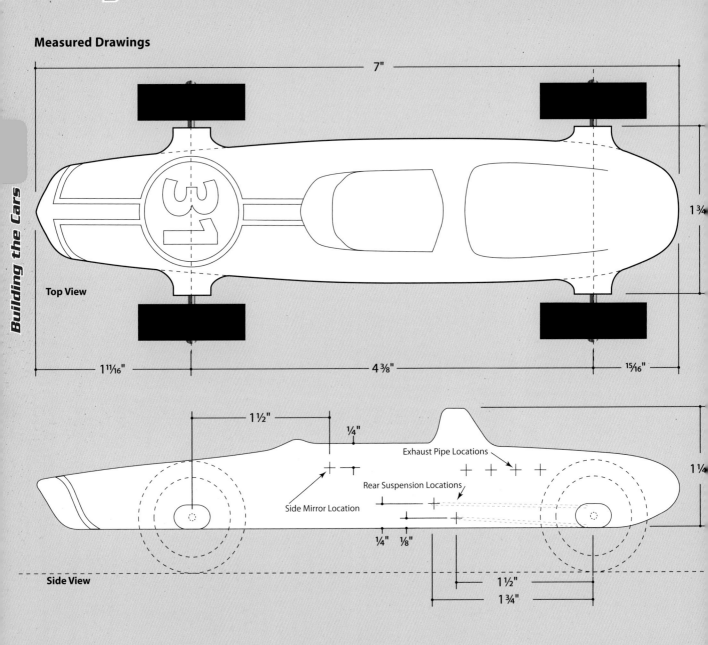

Top View

7"

1 ¾"

1¹¹⁄₁₆"   4³⁄₈"   ¹⁵⁄₁₆"

Side View

1½"

¼"

Exhaust Pipe Locations

Rear Suspension Locations

Side Mirror Location

¼" ⅛"

1¼"

1½"

1¾"

Cutting Pattern

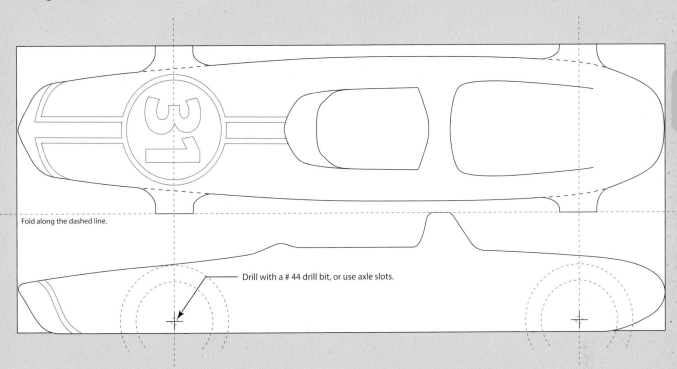

Fold along the dashed line.

Drill with a # 44 drill bit, or use axle slots.

Engine Patterns

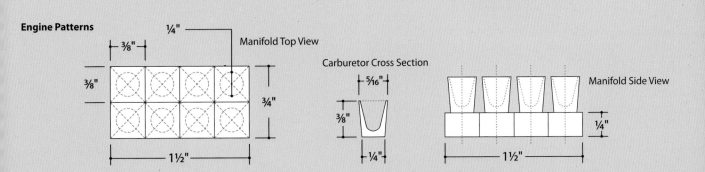

¼"

Manifold Top View

⅜"

⅜"

¾"

1½"

Carburetor Cross Section

5⁄16"

⅜"

¼"

Manifold Side View

1½"

¼"

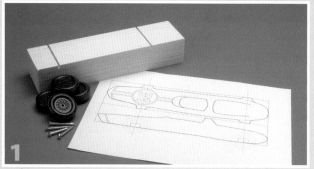

1 Make a few copies of the Cutting Pattern on page 43. Make sure your rules allow you to drill new axle holes. The provided axle slots tend to split when you pound the axles into the block because you'll have removed a large quantity of material around the axle slots.

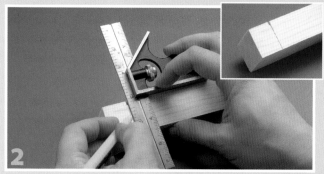

2 If you are drilling new axle holes, flip the block from the kit over. Then, use a square and the pattern to transfer the location of the axle slots to the other side. If you are using the standard axle slots, skip ahead to Step 4.

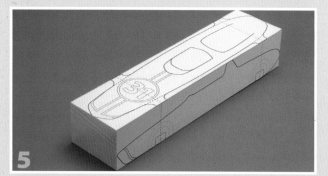

3 Clamp the block in place if needed. Measure and drill the holes with a drill press or use a Derby Worx axle-drilling jig. Slide the jig on the block and line up the jig's centerline. Drill both sides before moving the jig. Using a #44 drill bit will result in perfectly drilled holes.

4 Cut out one copy of the pattern with scissors and fold it along the long dashed line.

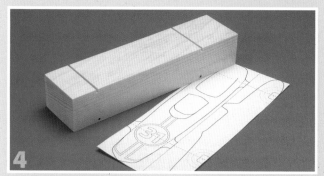

5 Spray the back of the pattern with spray mount. (Be sure to spray the pattern and not the wood.) Carefully attach the pattern to the block, as shown.

6 Use a scroll saw or the saw of your choice to cut the side profile of the car. Once you have finished cutting, do not discard the waste pieces.

7 Reattach the trimmed pieces using 1"-wide painter's tape so that the top profile of the pattern is ready to be cut.

8 Then, cut the top profile with the saw of your choice.

9 Reapply the tape to hold the top profile of the pattern on the block as parts are cut off.

10 Once all of the cuts are made, remove the tape and the extra pieces. Your car should now look like this.

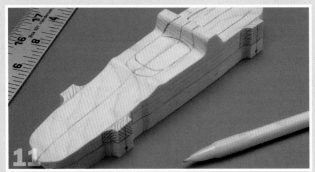

11 Draw a centerline down the top, bottom, and side profiles. Also, use the Cutting Pattern to draw the cockpit, headrest, and engine deck. I have marked the areas above the axle holes that should be removed.

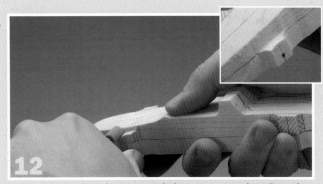

12 Using a cylinder-shaped tungsten carbide cutter mounted in a Dremel tool, make light passes to slowly remove the material in the shaded area down to the side profile centerline. The inset photo shows the final result.

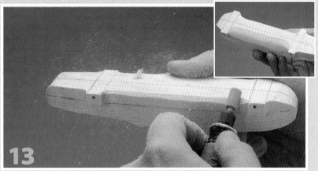

13 On the bottom, round the area between the axles from the side centerline to the bottom centerline using the cylinder-shaped tungsten carbide cutter. Round both sides. Be careful not to remove the wood around the axle holes.

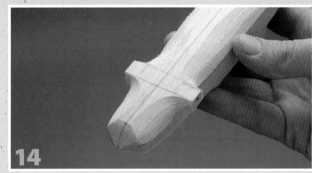

14 Round the area in front of the front axles using the same lines, as shown.

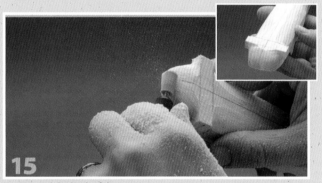

15 Next, round the back of the car.

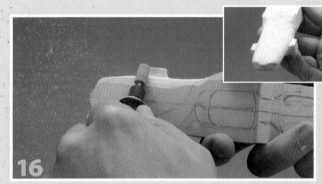

16 Round the top of the car from the front edge of the cockpit to the nose.

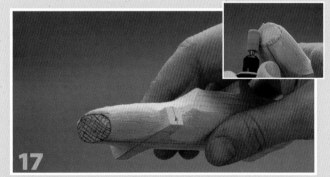

17 Mark the area of the grill to be removed. Slowly remove the material, being careful not to remove the top edge.

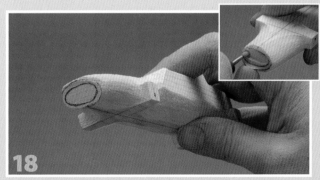

18 Draw the inner edge of the grill on the car. Using a small high speed cutter in the shaping tool, slowly remove the material. Cut up to the line, but do not remove it. Cut the recess about ³⁄₁₆" deep.

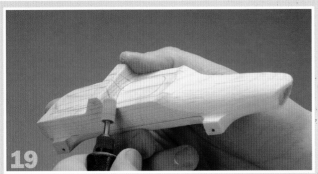

19 Round the side and rear of the car from the side of the cockpit to the rear of the car.

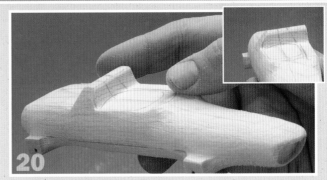

20 Start to round the headrest, as shown.

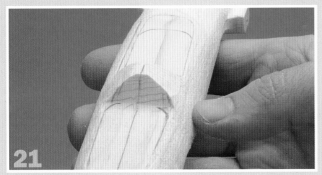

21 Finish rounding the headrest.

22 Using the small high speed cutter, create a concave area in the back of the headrest.

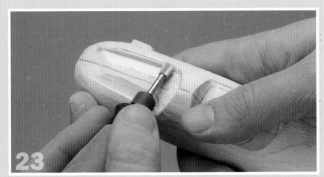

23 Using a large high speed cutter in the shaping tool, remove the material on the rear engine deck.

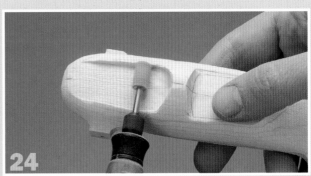

24 Use the cylinder-shaped tungsten carbide cutter to smooth out the area.

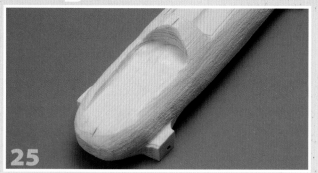

25 Once it has been smoothed out, the engine deck should look like this.

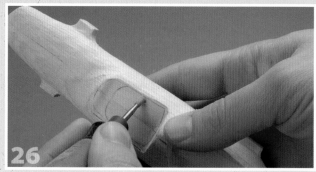

26 Start forming the cockpit by cutting a recessed area ⅛" deep along the outer line with the small high speed cutter.

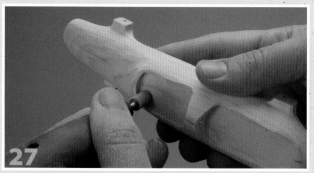

27 Next, smooth the area with the large high speed cutter.

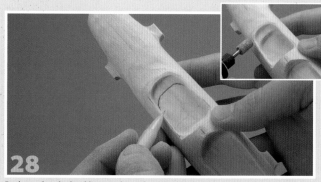

28 Redraw the dashed line and cut the remaining area ¼" deep with the cylinder-shaped tungsten carbide cutter.

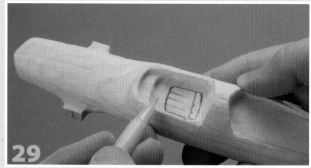

29 Roughly draw the seat and seat back in the cockpit. Leave ⅛" between the seat and the headrest.

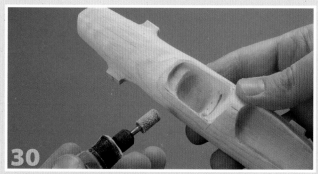

30 Continue cutting the recess to ½" deep from the back of the seat to the dashboard with the cylinder-shaped tungsten carbide cutter.

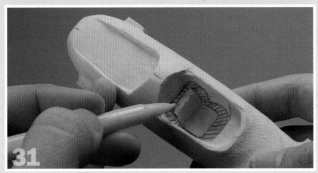

31 Mark the area around the seat that will be removed.

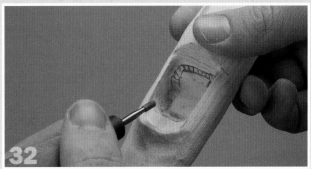

32 Use the small high speed cutter to cut the floor of the cockpit ⅛" deeper. Carefully remove the material around the seat.

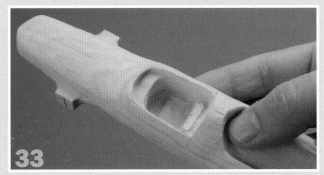

33 With the material around the seat removed, the cockpit should look like this.

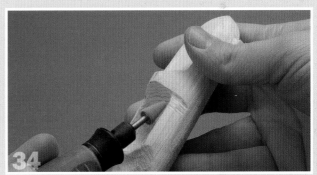

34 Next, thin the sides of the cockpit with a cone-shaped tungsten carbide cutter mounted in the shaper tool.

35 Leave an edge of material between the back edge of the cockpit and the sides of the headrest.

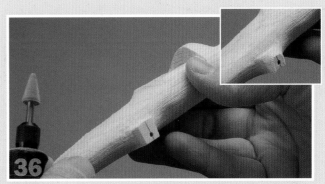

36 Round the axle area using the cone-shaped tungsten carbide cutter. The inset shows what the area should look like. Do all four the same way.

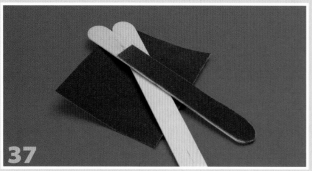

37

Spray mount 120-grit sandpaper to a craft stick to block sand the car and flatten any high spots.

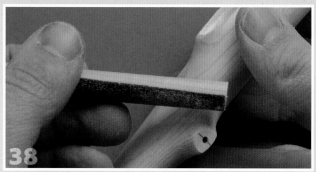

38

Wrap 120-grit sandpaper around a ⅜" dowel to sand hard-to-reach concave areas.

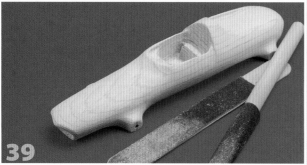

39

Continue sanding the car with 120-grit sandpaper until all the sides are flat.

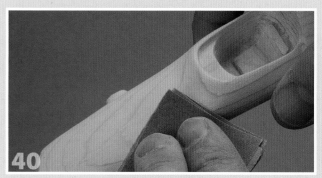

40

Next, hand sand the car with 220-grit sandpaper.

41

Look over the car and make any final adjustments to the body. At this point, the car body is complete. Now we are ready to add the details.

42

Clamp a power drill in a bench vise. Cut a ⅜" dowel to 3" in length. Then, insert the dowel and secure it tightly in the drill.

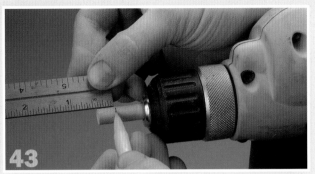

43 Measure ⅜" from the end and draw a line as a reference point.

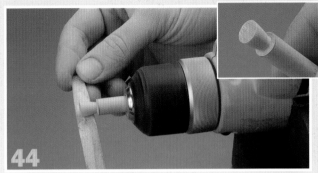

44 Using a small flat file, taper the end of the dowel to form the outside of the carburetor. Taper the base of the carburetor to about ¼".

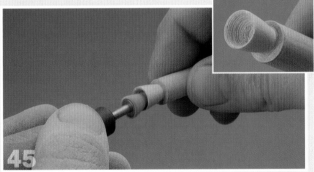

45 Open the inside of the carburetor with the cone-shaped tungsten carbide cutter mounted in the shaper tool. Start in the center and slowly work the cutter deeper.

46 Use a coping saw to cut the carburetor from the dowel.

47 Lightly sand the bottom of the carburetor with 220-grit sandpaper so it will sit on a flat surface. Repeat Steps 42 to 47 seven times to make a total of eight carburetors.

48 From scrap wood, cut a piece that measures 1½" x ¾" x ³⁄₁₆". This will become the intake manifold to which you'll attach the eight carburetors. Draw a ⅜" grid on the surface and sides. The diagonal lines mark the center of each carburetor.

49 Measure the bottom of your carburetor. Use a circle template to mark the exact location where you will attach each one. Draw curved lines between the circles, as shown in the inset photo.

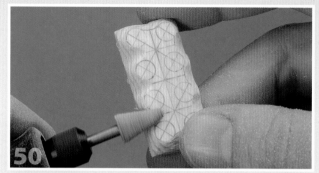

50 Using the cone-shaped tungsten carbide cutter, cut between the edges of the intake manifold and the carburetor reference marks. The goal is to round the intake without removing the wood where the carburetor will be glued. Hand sand until smooth with 220-grit sandpaper.

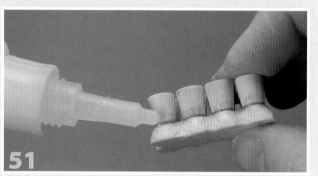

51 Glue each carburetor to the manifold with CA glue. Make sure they are attached exactly in the center of the marked location. After the glue dries, put a bead of glue around the base of the carburetor to fill any gaps.

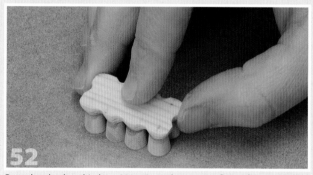

52 Once the glue has dried, set 220-grit sandpaper on a flat surface and lightly sand the tops of the carburetors to make them even across the top.

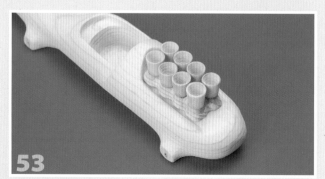

53 Dry fit the completed engine assembly on the car. Don't glue it into position yet.

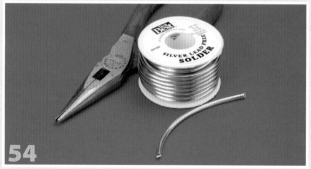

54 To begin building the exhaust pipes, cut eight 4"-long pieces of lead-free plumbing repair solder with wire cutters. Plumbing solder is available at any home center. It should be approximately ⅛" in diameter.

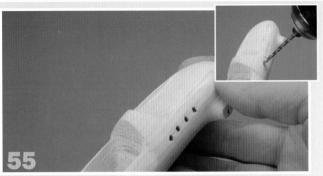

Mark the eight locations of the exhaust pipes using the Measured Drawing on page 42. Drill ⅛" holes perpendicular to the side of the car about ½" deep.

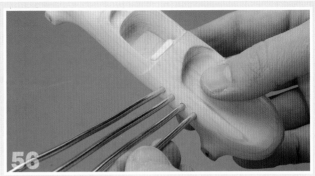

Insert the wires into the holes, but do not glue them yet.

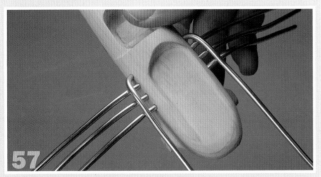

Bend the front wire over the top of the other wires.

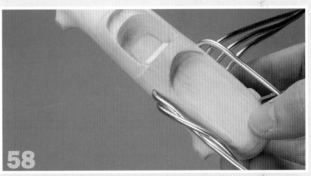

Next, bend the second wire over the top of the first wire. Continue with the third and fourth wires. Bend each wire around the previous wires toward the rear of the car. Do this on both sides. The pipes will be a mirror image of each other.

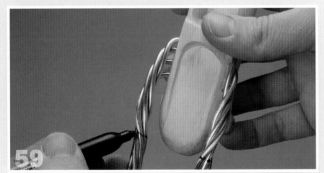

Using a black marker, such as a Sharpie, put a mark on the pipes that is even with the end of the car. It is very important that the pipes do not stick out past the end of the car. The car will be disqualified if it is over 7" long.

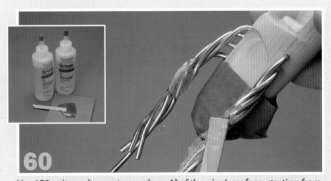

Use 120-grit sandpaper to rough up 1" of the pipe's surface, starting from the mark and moving toward the front of the car. Mix a small amount of 5-minute epoxy and spread it around the rough area. Protect the back of the car with painter's tape.

61 Let the epoxy fully cure. Then, use a 1¼" cut-off wheel mounted in the shaping tool to trim the exhaust pipes at the premarked area. Don't forget to wear safety glasses and a dust mask.

62 A ½" 60-grit sanding drum mounted in the shaping tool quickly smoothes out the epoxy.

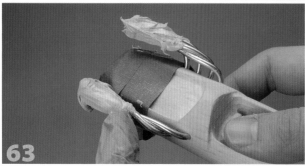

63 Mix a small amount of wood filler, such as Bondo, and spread it around the pipes. Let it dry completely. Follow the manufacturer's directions for drying time, and be sure to wear gloves when working with this product.

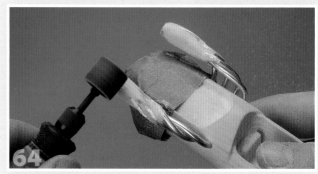

64 Start with the ½" sanding drum to quickly smooth the filler. You want the rear of the pipes to have a round, tubelike shape. Finish smoothing the filler with 220-grit sandpaper.

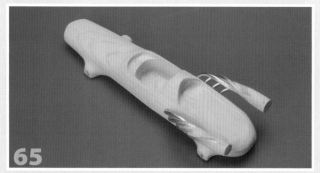

65 Here are the finished exhaust pipes. Make sure you carefully remove the pipes before painting.

66 To start building the roll bar, cut a piece of plumbing solder about 2½" long. Form the top of the roll bar around a round object such as the handle of a small round file.

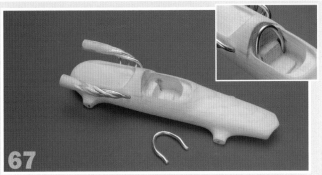

67 Select a drill bit that is the same diameter as the solder. I used a ⅛" drill bit for this step. Drill a hole along each side of the seat. Test fit the roll bar and trim it so it is the same height as the wooden headrest. Do not glue the roll bar in place at this time.

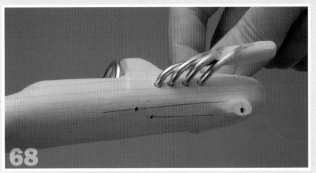

68 Mark the location of the holes for the rear suspension using the Measured Drawings on page 42. Drill ¹⁄₁₆"-diameter holes approximately ½" deep.

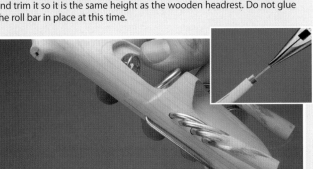

69 Cut a 16" piece of 14-gauge electrical ground wire. Pull the uncoated ground wire from the protective outer casing and discard the rest. Cut the wire into four 4" pieces. Insert each piece of wire into the predrilled holes and bend them back toward the rear axle hole.

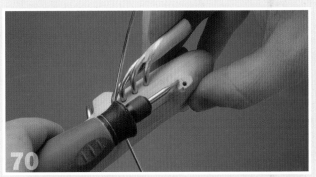

70 Mark the location where the wire touches the wood around the rear axle. Cut the wire to length with wire cutters. Then, use the shaping tool with the small high speed cutter to cut grooves in the wood.

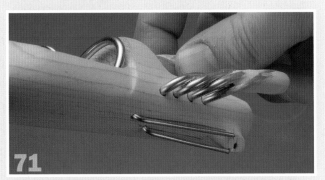

71 Cut each groove deep enough so the wire is completely level with the wood around the axle area. Continue until all four rear suspension wires are in place. Do not glue them at this time.

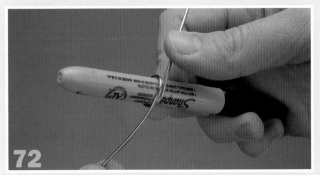

72 To make the steering wheel, start with a piece of 14-gauge electrical ground wire. Wrap it once around a round object. A black marker works well.

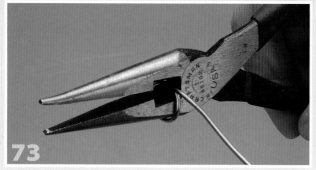

73

Slide the wire off the marker. Use a pair of wire cutters to cut through both wires at the same time.

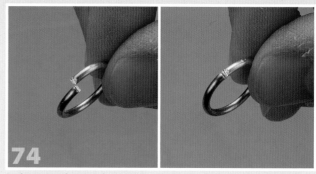

74

At this point, the wire should look as it does in the left photo. Carefully bend the ends of the ring together, so the wire looks as it does in the right photo.

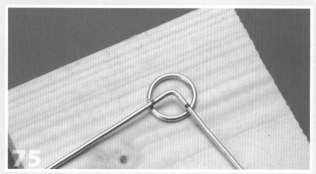

75

Bend a 90-degree angle in a piece of scrap wire. Lay the wire on the wire ring you just made and mark where it should be trimmed. Trim the wire with wire cutters.

76

Use a piece of painter's tape, with the sticky side up, to hold the parts together. Solder the wires together with a 40w soldering iron and electrical solder. Add a piece of straight wire to the back of the steering wheel. This step should be performed by an adult.

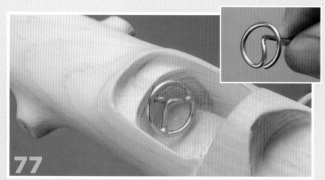

77

Sand the soldering joints smooth with the small round file and 220-grit sandpaper. Drill a 1/16" hole in the cockpit. Test fit the steering wheel and cut the shaft to the correct length. The wheel should be about 1/4" from the dash. If you want to make a simpler steering wheel, just bend a wire (see inset).

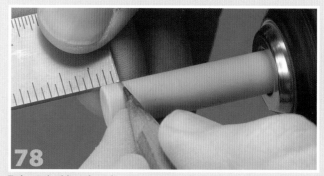

78

To begin building the side mirrors, cut a 3"-long 3/8" dowel and mount it in a power drill just as you did in Step 42. With the drill running, place a mark 3/16" from the end.

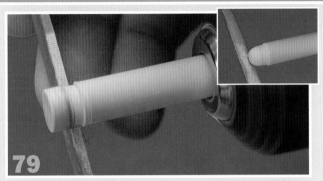

79 Use the side of the small flat file to cut a ¹⁄₁₆"-deep groove on the side of the line closer to the drill. Round the end of the dowel with the file. Stop the drill.

80 Drill a ¹⁄₁₆" hole in the mirror at a 30-degree angle approximately ¹⁄₈" deep.

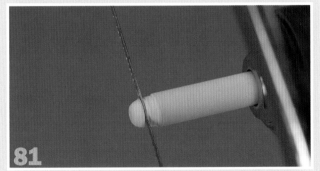

81 Turn the drill back on and cut the mirror from the dowel with a coping saw. Sand the flat part of the mirror smooth.

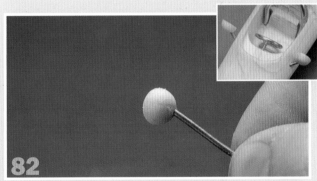

82 Using CA glue, attach the mirror to a piece of scrap 14-gauge wire. Drill the mirror holes in the car body, as marked on the Measured Drawings on page 42. Test fit the mirrors and trim the wire to the correct length. Bend the wire so the mirrors are perpendicular to the car body.

83 Test fit all of the pieces and make any adjustments as needed. This is how the completed car, before painting, should look. Add weight to the car before you begin the painting process (see "Adding Weight" on page 10 for more details).

Chapter 3
Painting Your Car

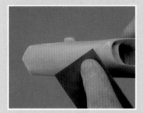   

Because of its impact on a project, painting and detailing intimidates many people. The finish you apply often makes or breaks a car design. If done poorly, it can turn a great design into an average one. Done well, it can turn a nice car into an outstanding car. This chapter shows techniques for getting great results every time. With a little patience and teamwork, you and your child can create an impressive finish together.

Before you begin, consider your skill level and that of your child and choose a paint type accordingly. Acrylic paint is great for beginners, while spray paint is best for experienced painters. No matter what type of paint you choose, be sure to follow the manufactor's instructions and work in a well-ventilated area. Remember to involve your child; encourage him to choose the colors and help with the actual painting process so he can make the car his own.

Painting the Vintage Racecar

The painting process for the Vintage Racecar is used as an example because it is the most complicated Derby car in this book, but you can apply these steps to any of the cars. Adding detail, pinstriping, and your favorite racecar number can really make your car stand out from the rest. Be creative, take your time during the process, and remember to wear a dust mask when working with these paints.

Materials and Tools

- Copies of Cutting Pattern, page 43
- Cardboard box 20" x 15" x 10" (for homemade spray painting booth)
- Second piece of cardboard 20" x 15" (for booth's bottom)
- Pencil
- Scissors
- Spray paint—primer, main color, trim color, metallic silver, black, and clear finish (all the same brand, such as Rust-Oleum®)
- Small bottles of flat black and silver enamel paint, such as Testors
- Small bottle of flat black acrylic paint
- Hobby knife
- Small paintbrush
- Extra axles or nails

- Fine wire or string
- Small piece of foam
- Wax paper
- Painter's tape
- Spray mount
- Cyanoacrylate (CA) glue
- Clear tape such as Scotch Magic Tape®
- 1/16" black pinstriping tape
- 220-grit sandpaper
- Several sheets of 400-grit wet/dry sandpaper
- Soft cloth
- Paper towels
- Small cup
- Safety glasses
- Dust mask
- Gloves

Painting Your Car

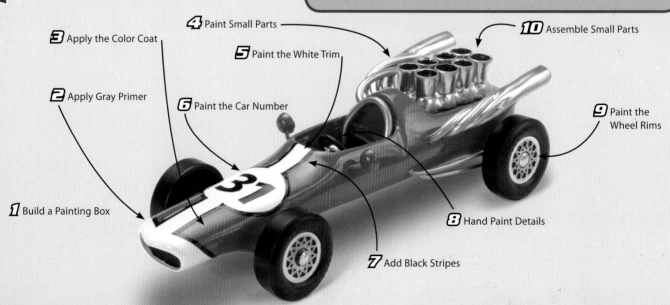

3 Apply the Color Coat

4 Paint Small Parts

5 Paint the White Trim

10 Assemble Small Parts

2 Apply Gray Primer

6 Paint the Car Number

9 Paint the Wheel Rims

1 Build a Painting Box

8 Hand Paint Details

7 Add Black Stripes

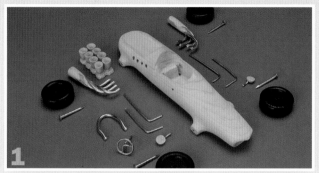

1 Lay out all of your pieces, and consider each one carefully. Sand off any rough spots with 220-grit sandpaper. A great paint job starts with a perfect surface. Remove any dust from the parts with a soft cloth.

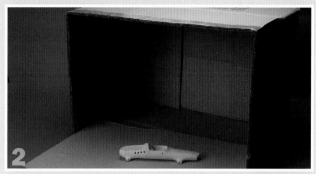

2 Start building a spray painting booth. This keeps spray paint from going where you don't want it. Open all of the flaps to a cardboard box and tape them vertically with painter's tape. Then, cut a second piece of cardboard to fit in the bottom of the box, as shown.

Making Spray Painting Easier for Children (and Adults)

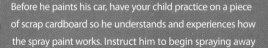

Getting a good paint job with a can of spray paint can be challenging for an adult, not to mention a child. If your child has trouble pressing and holding the nozzle down, try purchasing a snap-on handle to make it easier. These handles attach to the top of the spray bottles and are available at most home centers. The snap-on handle helps you or your child control the paint.

Before he paints his car, have your child practice on a piece of scrap cardboard so he understands and experiences how the spray paint works. Instruct him to begin spraying away from the car and then to sweep the paint past the car about 6" to 8" from the surface. Have him release the trigger after he passes the car. Remind him that if he points the can at the car and pulls the trigger, a large quantity of paint will hit one spot and cause a run in the finish. And always remember to be patient with mistakes.

You can help by holding the wire frame supporting the car while your child paints. If you see him applying too much paint, move the car away from the paint spray.

Encourage your child to take his time and use several light coats as opposed to one thick coat, which could result in runs and drips. Remember to wear a dust mask for protection against harmful fumes and to work in a well-ventilated area when spray painting.

Painting the Vintage Racecar

3 Tape a pencil to the top of the box, centering it along the top front edge. About 2" of the pencil should hang over the front edge.

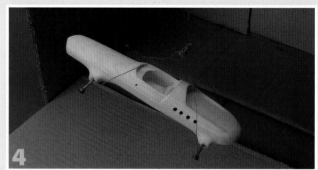

4 Insert extra axles ¼" into the Derby car. Wrap each axle with fine wire or string. Then, gather all of the wires above the car and twist them to form one wire. Hang the car from the pencil and make sure the wires don't touch the sides of the car.

5 Adjust the wire length to center the car in the middle of the box opening. This setup allows you to paint the top and the bottom of the car at the same time. Please check your local rules, however, because some packs require the bottom to be unpainted.

6 Select the colors you want. To avoid paint problems, use one brand of paint for all of the painting steps—priming, color coating, trim painting, and clear coating.

Oops . . . Don't Mix Brands of Spray Paint

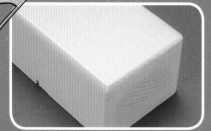

White Base Coat

Green Paint Reaction

Mixing different brands of spray paint can have disastrous results. In the photos at left, a sample block was sprayed with glossy white paint. After the white dried, the same block was sprayed with a different brand of satin green paint. The green paint crackled the white paint over the entire surface. If this happens on your finished car, you will need to resand the car down to the bare wood.

Painting Your Car

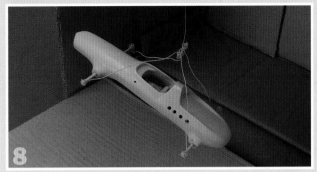

7 Select a good-quality primer. Begin by spraying a light coat of primer. Let it dry for about 30 minutes and then spray another, slightly heavier coat. Be sure to cover the bottom of your car with painter's tape if your local rules do not allow the bottom to be painted.

8 Add more coats of primer every 30 minutes until the entire car is covered. Allow the primer to dry for 2 hours.

9 Group all of the small parts in a piece of foam. Push the ends that don't need to be painted into the foam.

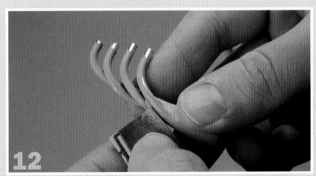

10 Spray the small parts with primer using the same process as Step 7 and 8.

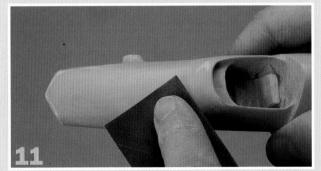

11 After the primer is dry, sand the car by hand with 400-grit wet/dry sandpaper. Refold the sandpaper as it becomes covered with removed paint. Sand the car dry; don't use water with the sandpaper because the wood will soak up the water and crack the paint.

12 Sand all of the small parts with 400-grit wet/dry sandpaper. Fold the paper to reach any tight areas.

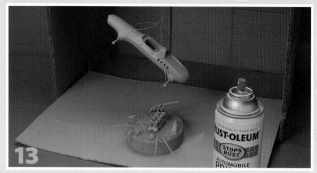

Spray another light coat of primer on all of the parts. Allow the primer to dry for 2 hours. Lightly sand the surfaces again with 400-grit wet/dry sandpaper.

Hang the car in the painting box. Spray a light coat of red paint or the color of your child's choice. Let it dry for about 30 minutes and then spray another, slightly heavier coat.

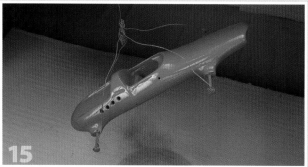

Continue to add more coats of colored paint every 30 minutes until the entire car is covered, and no more primer shows through. Allow the paint to dry overnight.

Spray the small parts with metallic silver paint. Allow the parts to dry for 2 hours.

Next, paint the side mirrors red. Parts too small to hold by hand can be held in painter's tape.

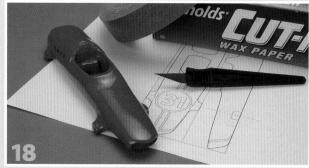

Once the car is dry, you're ready to paint the white trim. Gather the materials you'll need for making a painting mask for the car: wax paper, a copy of the Cutting Pattern on page 43, painter's tape, spray mount, scissors, and a hobby knife.

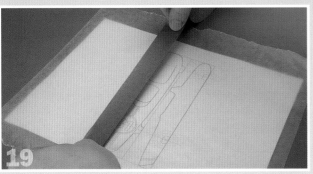

19 Lay a piece of wax paper over the Cutting Pattern. Place strips of painter's tape over the top panel of the pattern. Overlap each strip by 1/8".

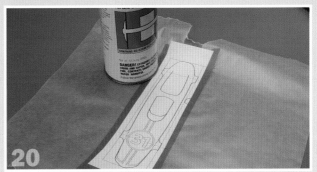

20 Remove the pattern from under the wax paper. Cut the top profile with a pair of scissors. Apply a light coat of spray mount to the bottom of the pattern and press it on top of the painter's tape.

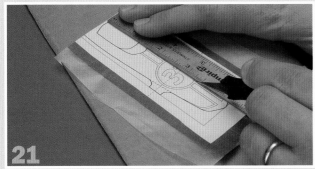

21 Cut all of the layers down to a smaller, more manageable size using a hobby knife. You need only the front of the car from the cockpit to the nose. Use a piece of scrap cardboard to protect the cutting surface.

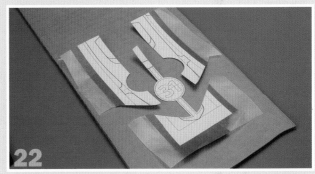

22 Use a hobby knife to trim along the outer edge of the design, as shown.

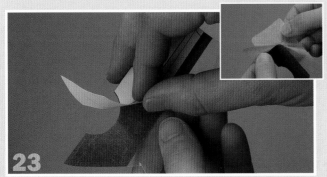

23 Peel the pattern from the painter's tape. Then, peel the painter's tape from the wax paper.

24 Apply the trimmed painter's tape pieces to the car, using the Cutting Pattern as reference. Firmly press the tape onto the car. Pay close attention to the trimmed edges. Any wrinkles will cause the paint to bleed under the tape.

25 Use painter's tape to complete the pattern on the underside.

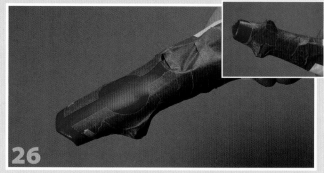

26 Cover the rest of the car with painter's tape and paper to protect the back of the car from overspray.

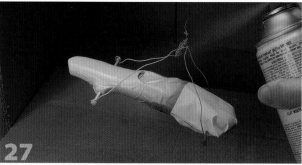

27 Double-check that all of the tape edges are pressed down. Spray the front of the car with glossy white paint or any color your child chooses. Allow the paint to dry for 2 hours.

28 Carefully remove all of the painter's tape.

29 Gather any materials you need for painting the number on the front of the car. For this process, use Scotch-brand Magic Tape. You can cut more complicated shapes using this particular tape.

30 Apply the tape to wax paper to cover the number "31" or the number that you chose on the pattern.

31

Spray mount the pattern on top of the Scotch tape.

32

Cut out the number with a hobby knife. Remember to cut on top of a piece of scrap cardboard. Remove the paper pattern.

33

Trim the template to about a 3" square.

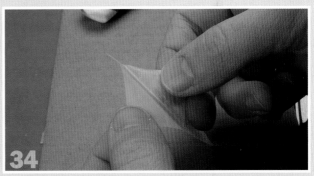

34

Peel off the tape template from the wax paper.

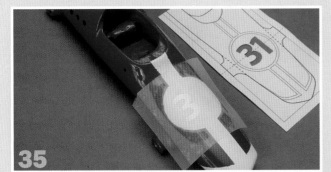

35

Position the template in the center of the white circle on the hood of the car.

36

Cut a 2" hole in the middle of a piece of paper. Lay the paper over the tape template and tape the paper in place with painter's tape. Spray the number with glossy black paint.

37

Remove the paper and then carefully peel off the tape template.

38

Any paint that bleeds under the tape template can be touched up. Spray the white paint into a small cup and use a small brush to hide any bleeding problems.

Painting the Raised Letters on BSA Wheels

To add flash, you can paint the raised letters on BSA wheels. This method, using a pointed toothpick to carefully trace the letters with enamel paint, produces great results.

Step 1: Round the very tip of a toothpick. A few passes on 220-grit sandpaper is all you need.

Step 2: Pour a small amount of paint into the paint cap.

Step 3: Dip the toothpick into the paint until just the tip has a dot of paint on it.

Step 4: If you're right-handed, start on the first letter in "Pinewood Derby" and continue until all of the letters are painted. If you accidentally fill in the insides of the letters, paint the insides flat black after the lettering paint has dried.

39

Use 1⁄16" black pinstriping tape to cover the red-to-white edge. If you can't find 1⁄16" black pinstriping tape, use the kind that comes with a thick and thin pinstripe. Any auto parts store will carry a wide range of sizes and colors.

40

Cut an 8" piece of black pinstriping tape. Remove the thin stripe and position it over the red paint just to the white edge. Apply the stripe slowly and press down firmly as you work the tape around the curve.

41

Use a hobby knife to trim the black stripes to length.

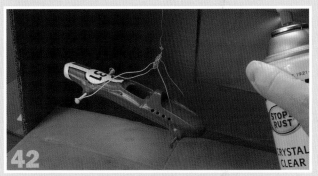

42

To keep the pinstripes from peeling back, spray a few coats of clear coat over the car body. Do not spray clear coat over the silver parts. Metallic paint and clear coat react poorly with each other. Allow paint to dry for 2 hours.

43

Once the clear coat is dry, you're ready to hand paint details. To start, paint the dash and the seat with flat black enamel paint, such as Testors, and a small paintbrush.

44

Paint the back of the grill opening.

45 Use a small paintbrush to paint the insides of the carburetors.

46 Wipe off any paint on the top edge.

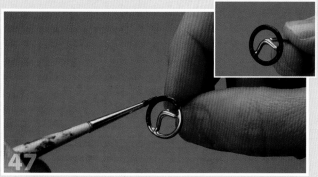

47 Paint the outside of the steering wheel with the flat black paint.

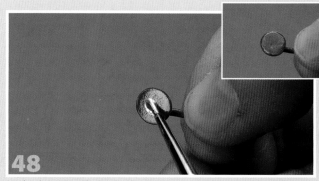

48 Apply silver enamel paint, such as Testors, to the flat part of the mirrors.

49 Decide if you want to paint the spokes of the BSA wheels. This step adds extra detail to your car. If you choose to paint the spokes, apply painter's tape over the entire wheel. If you choose to leave the spokes as is, skip ahead to Step 55.

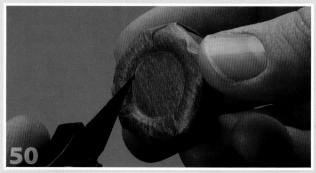

50 Press the tape into the edges of the rim. Use a hobby knife to carefully cut around the edge of the rim.

51

Peel the tape from the center of the wheel. Spray the wheel with silver spray paint, such as Rust-Oleum Bright Coat Metallic Finish. Allow the paint to dry completely.

52

Brush flat black acrylic paint into the wire pattern. Use a damp paper towel to remove the paint from the high areas.

53

Wipe the wire pattern clean with a dry paper towel. If you removed too much black paint from the deep areas, reapply the black paint and try again.

54

Remove the painter's tape, and you are ready to assemble the car.

55

Lay out all of the car's parts. Use a small amount of CA glue to attach the parts to the car body. Do not glue the axles and wheels in place yet.

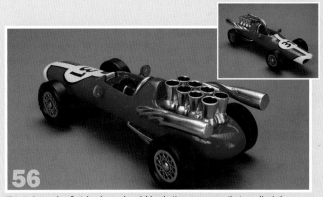

56

This is how the finished car should look. I've temporarily installed the axles and wheels. Follow the directions on pages 78–83 to prepare the axles and wheels properly before you permanently install them.

Creating Custom Decals

Materials and Tools

- Decals of choice
- Scissors
- Bowl of warm water
- Paper towels
- Spray clear coat
- Dust mask

You may purchase Pinewood Derby decals from an online retailer, such as *www.scoutstuff.org,* or you can create custom decals from your home ink-jet printer. If you choose to print your own, simply scan the decal patterns supplied in this book, or scan the patterns of your choice, and then print them on special decal transfer paper (see the Resources section on page 118 for details). Be sure to follow the manufacturer's printing directions. The step-by-step instruction shown here provides tips on applying the decals to the car. Remember, encourage your child to express his creativity at this stage—let him pick and place the decals for his car.

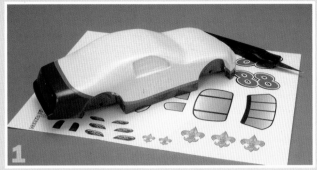

1

Print out the decals you've chosen. Homemade decals work best on white cars. Ink-jet printers can't print white ink so the decals are very transparent.

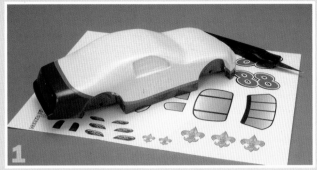

2

Trim around each decal with scissors, leaving about ⅟₁₆" all the way around. Your trimmed decal should look like the one in the inset.

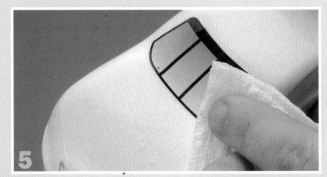

3

Soak the decal in a bowl of warm water. It will roll up and then slowly unroll in about 30 seconds. After that, the decal will slide off the backing material. Slightly slide the decal off the backing.

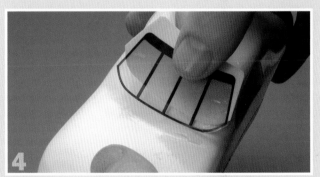

4

Position the decal on the car and slowly finish sliding the backing material away.

5

Use a paper towel to press the decal onto the car body.

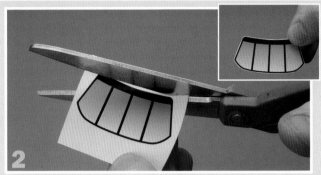

6

After you have added all of the decals, spray the entire car with a few coats of spray clear coat to help prevent the decals from coming off the car.

Using an Airbrush

Airbrushes are useful tools for producing special designs, such as the popular hot rod flames, but they can be difficult to control if you are painting freehand. However, by applying the technique shown here, it's easy to ensure excellent results. Small, affordable airbrushes are available from stores that carry model paints. (See pages 100-103 for instructions and patterns for building the Hot Rod Coupe shown here.)

(See pages 100-103 for instructions and patterns for building the Hot Rod Coupe shown here.)

Materials and Tools

- ■ **Airbrush**
- ■ **Yellow, orange, red, and white enamel paints or colors of choice**
- ■ **Paint thinner**
- ■ **Hobby knife**
- ■ **Liquid mask or painter's tape**
- ■ **Fine-line marker, such as a Sharpie**
- ■ **Spray clear coat**
- ■ **Safety glasses**
- ■ **Dust mask**

Thin the paint before you begin by mixing it with an equal part of paint thinner. Inexpensive starter airbrushes use a can of compressed air as the propellant for the paint. If the paint is not thinned, it will clog the spray tip of the airbrush.

Cover your car with liquid mask or painter's tape. Then, draw or trace the pattern on page 75 onto the car with a fine-line marker. Carefully cut out the area you want to paint with a hobby knife. Cut only through the paint mask; do not cut into the car. Remove the mask from the area you want to paint.

Spray a base coat of yellow over the entire flame area. I suggest practicing on a scrap piece to see how fast the paint comes out before trying it on the car.

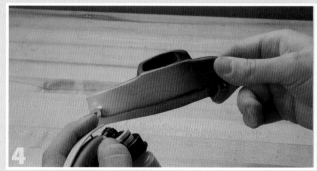

Lightly spray orange from the middle of the flame to the tips.

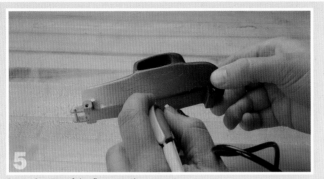

Spray the tips of the flames red.

Spray the front of the flames white. Carefully remove all of the liquid mask or painter's tape. After the paint is dry, spray a clear coat over the entire car.

Flame paint templates

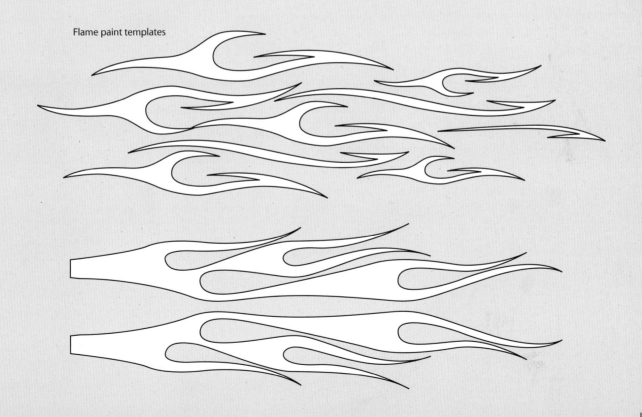

Chapter 4
Getting Ready for the Race

In this chapter, you'll see how easy it is to polish the axles and wheels so your Derby car will not only look great but also race like a rocket. You will also learn proper wheel attachment and spacing, which is key to winning a Derby race. The final section discusses the best ways to involve your child in race day activities.

Polishing the Axles

Axles straight from the kit have a set of small burrs, or imperfections, below the axle head. If you leave these burrs on your axles, they will create friction whenever the wheel and the axle head touch, which will slow down your car. The axle head also contains burrs, so it must be polished smooth as well.

Your child can perform most of the work in these steps—with your supervision, of course. Make sure he understands why each step is necessary and try to make the process fun.

Materials and Tools

- **Dremel tool or power drill**
- **Small triangular file**
- **400-, 600-, and 1000-grit wet/dry sandpaper**
- **Small dish of water**
- **Safety glasses**
- **Dust mask**

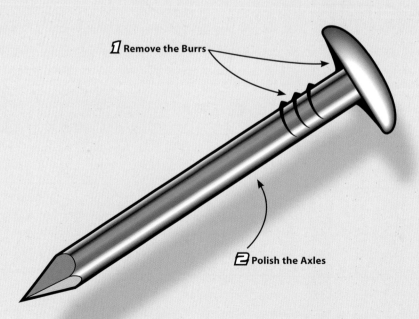

1 **Remove the Burrs**

2 **Polish the Axles**

1 Insert an axle into a shaper tool or a power drill, leaving about ⅝" exposed. Notice the burrs.

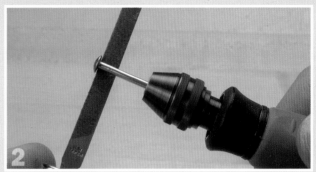

2 Turn the shaper tool or drill on low speed. Then, use a small triangular file to remove the burrs. Use light pressure on the file so you do not damage the axle.

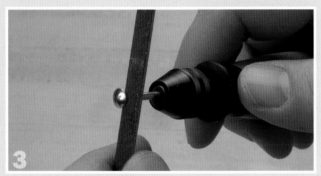

3 Rotate the file to remove the burrs under the axle head.

4 Keep different grits of wet/dry sandpaper handy. Use a sheet of 400-grit sandpaper to start, and cut a small strip about ¼" wide and 3" long. Dip the strip into a small dish of water.

5 Apply sandpaper to the axle. Sand the entire axle, including the inside surface of the head. This step should take about 15 seconds.

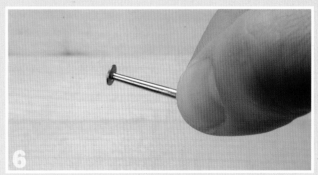

6 Repeat the process using 600- and 1000-grit sandpaper. When you're finished sanding, your axles should look like this.

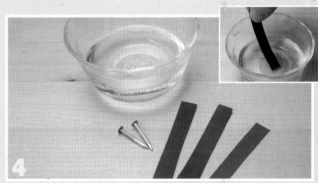

Polishing the Axles

Polishing the Wheels

Official BSA wheels, straight from the box, sometimes have undesirable features, such as large divots or bubbles. They can also have other abnormalities that will reduce the speed of your car if left intact. The very basic steps of wheel preparation, outlined in this section, will rid your wheels of these defects. Remember to check your local rules and regulations before modifying wheels.

To perform these techniques, you need a wheel mandrel. This handy tool is available at most Official BSA Scout Shops®, hobby stores, and Pinewood Derby online stores. Do not sand your wheels without a wheel mandrel because you will end up with wheels that are not perfectly round.

Materials and Tools

- Dremel tool or other shaping tool or power drill
- Wheel mandrel, such as the Derby Worx model
- 600-grit wet/dry sandpaper
- Flat block of wood or sanding block
- Small dish of water
- Graphite
- Soft cloth
- Safety glasses
- Dust mask

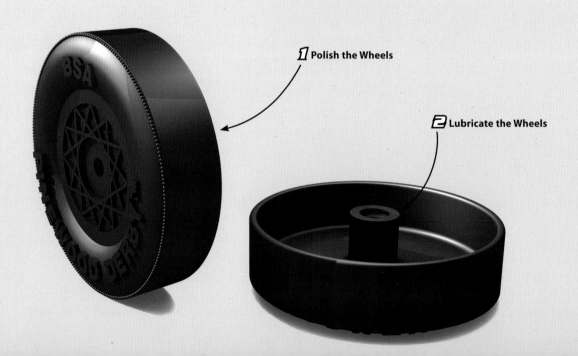

1 Polish the Wheels

2 Lubricate the Wheels

Attach a wheel to a mandrel, such as this one from Derby Worx. Then, place the mandrel in a shaper tool or a power drill.

Attach a small sheet of 600-grit wet/dry sandpaper to a flat block of wood or a sanding block. Moisten the sandpaper with water.

Turn on the shaper tool or the drill and set it at low speed. Allow the spinning wheel to gently rub against the sandpaper. Add more water when the paper starts to look dry. If you don't keep the sandpaper damp and maintain minimal pressure, the plastic will become hot and melt.

Constantly monitor the pressure that you apply. Too much will create a deformed wheel.

Sand until the mold bubble is gone and the wheel looks smooth.

Put a small amount of graphite onto a soft cloth. Polish the wheel with the graphite cloth until your wheel shines. Make sure you wear a dust mask and safety glasses when working with graphite.

Attaching the Wheels

Once your axles and wheels are polished, you're ready to attach the wheels. Attachment and spacing are extremely important. If the wheel and the car body are too far apart, the wheels will shake and wobble. If they are too close, the wheel hub will rub against the car. In this section, I'll show you an easy way to get the spacing right every time.

- ■ **2 or 3 business cards**
- ■ **White glue**
- ■ **Tape measure or ruler**
- ■ **Scissors**
- ■ **Graphite**
- ■ **Small dish**
- ■ **Small paintbrush**
- ■ **Safety glasses**
- ■ **Dust mask**

1 Glue two or three business cards together (enough to equal ⅟₃₂" thick) with white glue. Use a tape measure or ruler to make sure your stack of cards is the proper thickness.

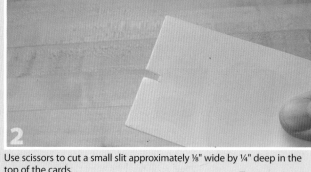

2 Use scissors to cut a small slit approximately ⅛" wide by ¼" deep in the top of the cards.

3 Attach each wheel to the car (they should stay in place without any adhesive) using the spacer you just made to control the space between the wheel and the car body.

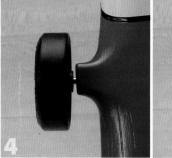

4 Adjust your wheel until it is spaced properly, like the one in the left photo. The right photo shows an improperly spaced wheel.

Once all four wheels are attached, place the car on a flat surface. Position yourself so you can look directly underneath the car. If any of the wheels do not rest flat and square on the surface, adjust them until they do.

To apply graphite to the wheel bore, put a small amount from the tube into a small dish. Dip a small paintbrush into the graphite, and then gently transfer the graphite from the brush to the wheel bore.

Using Graphite

Always wear a dust mask when using graphite. Because graphite particles are very light, they can become suspended in the air, where they can be inhaled. Graphite also tends to get everywhere and on everything. To contain the graphite, find a suitable place to work outside or cover your working surface with newspaper, cloth, or plastic.

As you apply the graphite, gently shake or tap each wheel to help move the graphite farther into the wheel bore. Remember to wear a dust mask and safety glasses whenever you work with graphite.

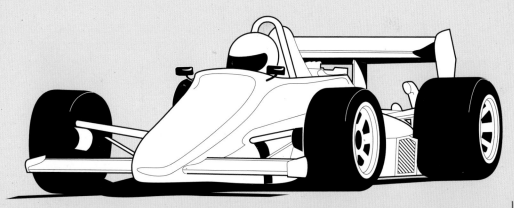

The Final Weigh-In

Before you show up at the check-in station on race day, ensure that your child's car isn't too heavy. Add extra weight if desired, and practice weighing the car with your child.

Checking the car's weight is especially important. If your car is over the weight limit on race day, you must remove excess weight or you won't be allowed to race, and making modifications at the race can be tricky. Before the race, weigh the car on a small digital scale or take it to your local post office and ask them to weigh it for you. Then, make any necessary adjustments. Aim for about 4.95 ounces.

If the car is underweight and you want it to be exactly 5.0 ounces, follow the step-by-step directions here for adding a small amount of weight. It's best to drill the hole at home and complete the other steps at weigh-in, but you can perform all of the steps at the race if necessary. If you don't have a power drill, which is used in the demonstration, you can still add extra weight by screwing brass screws into the bottom of the car.

Last but not least, let your child weigh-in his car. At most weigh-ins, parents line up to place their "child's" car on the scale, but it's better to let your child place his own car on the scale. If you use the method for adding extra weight, practice with your child at home. Put your scale on the table and have your child carefully place the car on the scale—upside down so that it won't roll off—and then add small weights to the scale until it reads 5.0 ounces. That way, when you show up at weigh-in, your child will know exactly what to do.

Materials and Tools

- **Power drill with ⅜" bit**
- **Small weights of choice**
- **CA glue**
- **Safety glasses**
- **Dust mask**
- **Gloves**

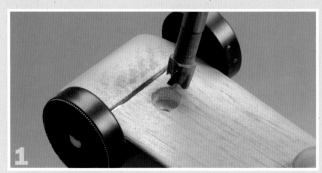

Drill a ⅜" hole in the bottom of the car with a power drill, being careful not to get sawdust on or around the axles or wheels.

Have your child place the car upside down on the scale and slowly add weights until the scale reads 5.0 ounces. Small split shot fishing weights, tungsten putty, and modeling clay fit easily into the small hole you drilled. If you use any lead products, follow safety precautions during and after their use (see page 9).

Use CA glue to keep the weights in place. Again, be careful not to get any glue near the axles and wheels.

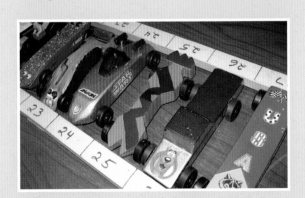

Your Derby car can take on a variety of shapes, sizes and colors (at right) and be a big hit on race day. Whatever your design, though, the key is to have fun as these families did on race day (above and below).

FAST TRACK
FINISH

1/16"

7/8"

2⅞"

4⅜"

4"

Extra Wheel No...
and Glue to t...

⅝"

Side View

1¼"

Remove this Material
with a Dremel Tool

3/8"

1½"

5/8"

Left Front Fender
Pattern

Right Front Fend...
Pattern

Pattern Portfolio

This pattern portfolio contains 31 amazing patterns and designs to help you and your child create your own sleek-looking Pinewood Derby car. In the first section, beginner, intermediate, and advanced design profiles help you generate your own ideas depending on the size car you want. The second section features expanded designs—measured patterns, cutting patterns, tips, and reference photos— and provides guidance for building them. Additionally, the blank block patterns help you create any design you can dream up. Remember to keep the building and designing process fun and let your child's imagination run wild!

Beginner Designs

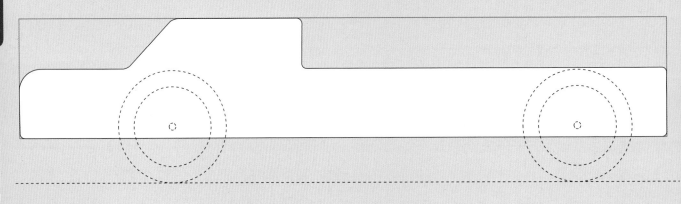

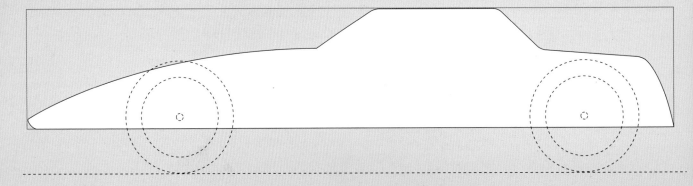

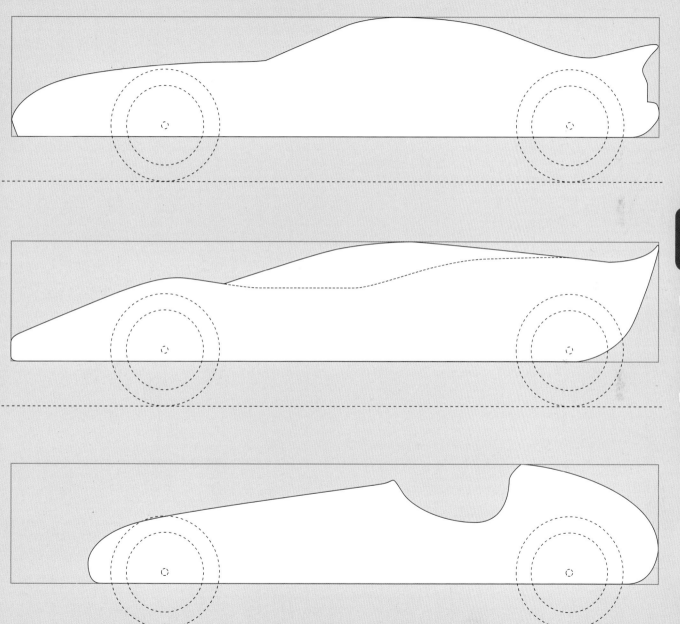

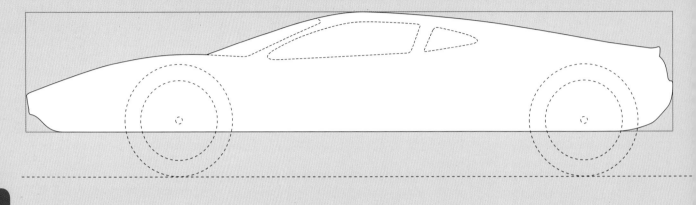

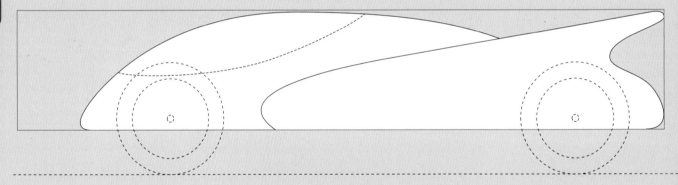

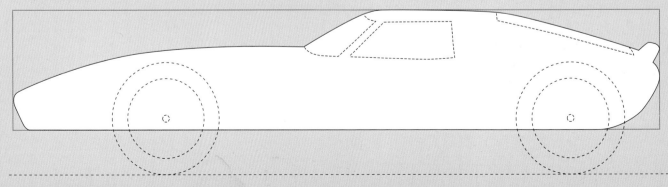

Intermediate Designs

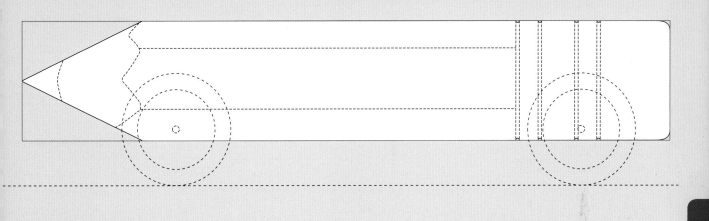

Speed Bus

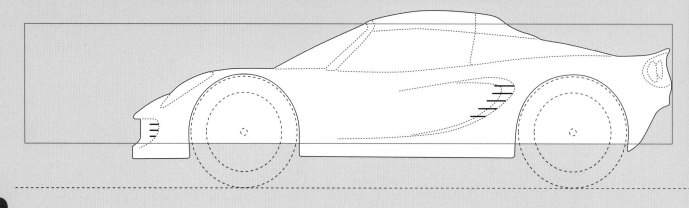

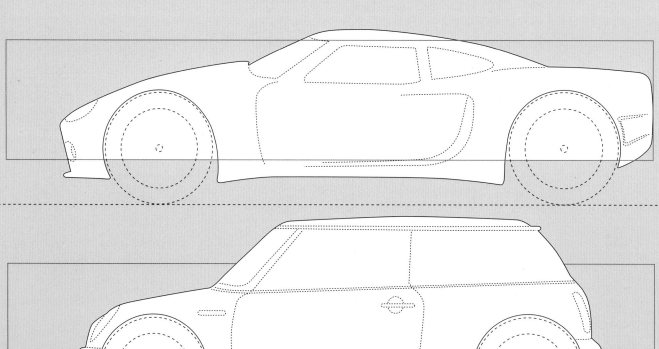

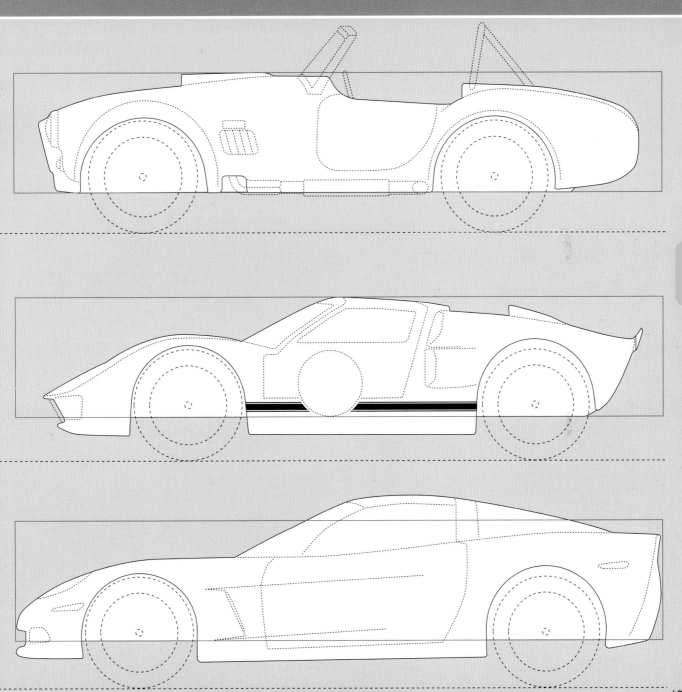

Army Jeep

Creating this advanced design is fun because it is not a typical Pinewood Derby car. It has a very short wheelbase and is a recognizable design that meets the Official Pinewood Derby specifications. Another feature is its very simple paint job. Because this car is so different from standard Derby designs, it may not be the fastest car. However, it will certainly be one of the best-looking.

Quick Tips

1 Flip the block over and drill new axle holes

2 Cut the main body from the BSA-supplied block

3 Attach the fenders to the main body

4 Attach wheel well blocks on the inside of the rear fenders

5 Remove the material under the front fenders

6 Glue the windshield to the main body

7 Bend wire to form two windshield posts and attach them to the windshield frame

8 Install the bumpers

9 Cut out the seats and shape them with a shaper tool

10 Build and install the steering wheel

11 Use a shaper tool to carefully carve the grill details and lights

12 Add the weights and fill in the holes

13 Sand the entire car smooth

14 Paint the main body and five wheel centers green

15 Paint the details (see pp. 59-75) and install the seats

16 Cut a notch in the bottom of the spare tire and glue it in place

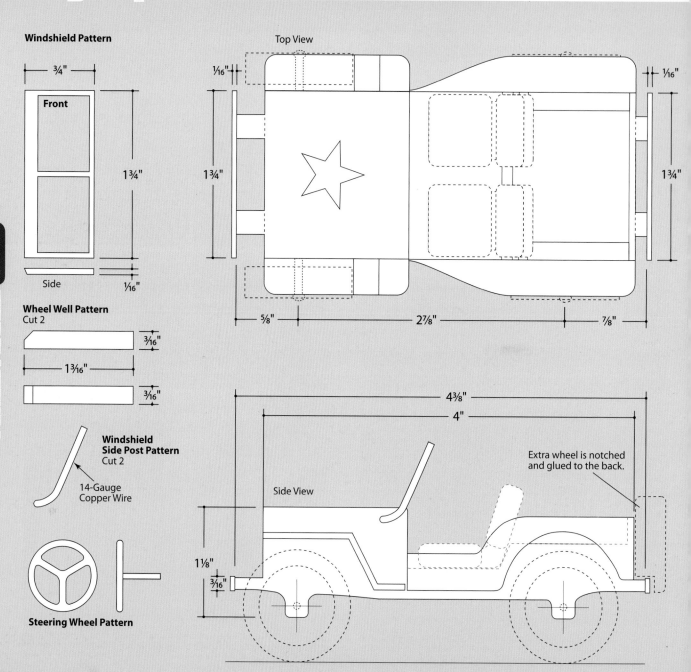

Windshield Pattern

¾"

Front

1¾"

Side

1/16"

Wheel Well Pattern
Cut 2

3/16"

1 3/16"

3/16"

**Windshield
Side Post Pattern**
Cut 2

14-Gauge
Copper Wire

Steering Wheel Pattern

Top View

1/16"

1¾"

1¾"

1/16"

5/8"   2⅞"   ⅞"

4⅜"

4"

Side View

Extra wheel is notched
and glued to the back.

1⅛"

3/16"

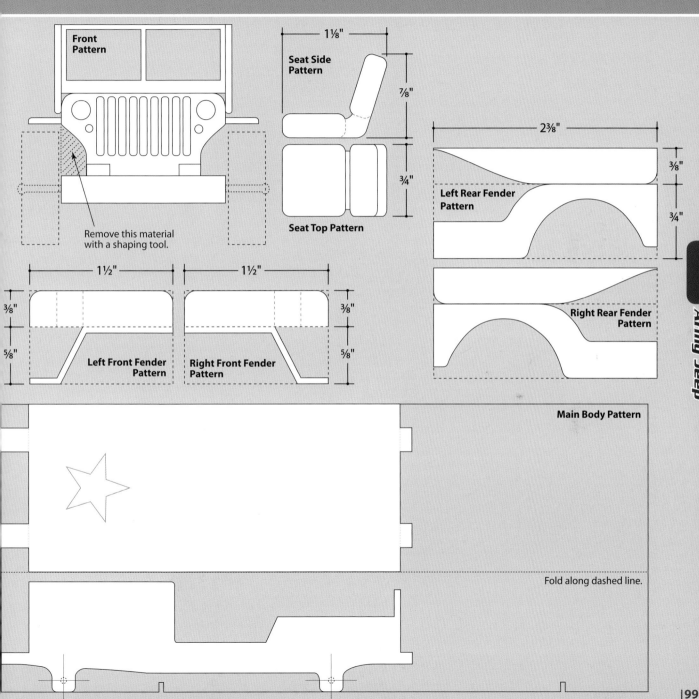

Front Pattern

Remove this material with a shaping tool.

Seat Side Pattern

1⅛"

⅞"

¾"

Seat Top Pattern

Left Rear Fender Pattern

2⅜"

⅜"

¾"

Right Rear Fender Pattern

Left Front Fender Pattern

1½"

⅜"

⅝"

Right Front Fender Pattern

1½"

⅜"

⅝"

Main Body Pattern

Fold along dashed line.

Army Jeep

Hot Rod Coupe

This relatively easy design looks fast even when sitting still. A ½" block of wood, added to the top of the BSA block, increases the car height. You'll need to remove material from the bottom of the car to create its aggressive stance. Its clean lines allow for many painting options—it looks great painted a solid color or works well with painted flames (see pages 74-75).

(see pages 74-75)

Quick Tips

1 Flip the block over and drill new axle holes

2 Attach a ½" block of wood to the top of the BSA block

3 Cut the side profile, and then cut the top profile

4 Remove the material above the front axles to form the hood sides

5 Drill a ⅛" hole and insert a ⅛" dowel in the front suspension

6 Use a shaper tool to cut open the front windshield

7 Add the weights and fill in the holes (see pp. 9-11)

8 Sand the entire car smooth

9 Paint with the color of your choice (see pp. 59-75)

10 Add flames (optional)

11 Apply clear coat

Measured Drawings

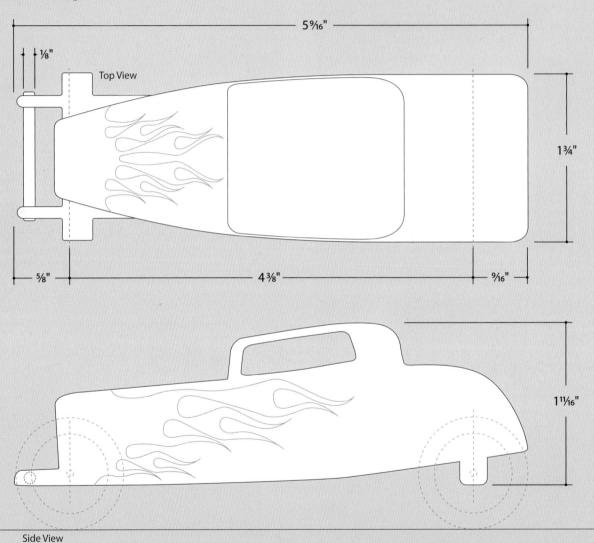

Top View

5⁹⁄₁₆"

1⁄₈"

1¾"

5⁄₈"

4³⁄₈"

⁹⁄₁₆"

1¹¹⁄₁₆"

Side View

Cutting Pattern

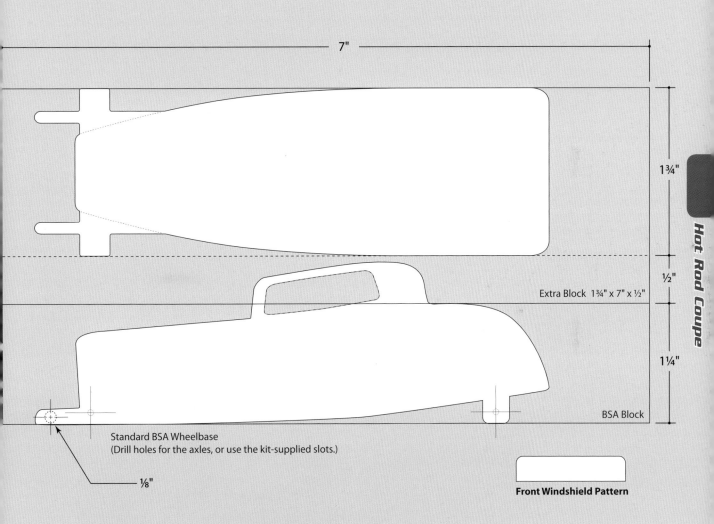

7"

1¾"

½"

Extra Block 1¾" x 7" x ½"

1¼"

BSA Block

Standard BSA Wheelbase
(Drill holes for the axles, or use the kit-supplied slots.)

⅛"

Front Windshield Pattern

Speed Swoop

My son and I have fine-tuned this simple design over the past few years and have trophies to prove its speed. The car is easy to cut from the supplied BSA block and features a very extended wheelbase and a light front end. To achieve maximum speed, place all of the weight over the rear axles. The super-simple design also makes this the easiest car to paint. To get a quick two-tone paint job, leave a square edge around the top of the car during the final sanding process. Then, paint the top the color you want. Let it dry, and cover the top with one piece of 1½"-wide painter's tape. Spray the bottom of the car another color (if local rules permit) and then peel off the tape.

Quick Tips

1 Flip the block over and drill new axle holes

2 Drill the weight holes before cutting out the car

3 Cut the side profile and then the top profile

4 Add the weights and fill in the holes (see pp. 9-11)

5 Sand the entire car smooth

6 Paint with the colors of your choice (see pp. 59-75)

7 Add decals (optional) (see pp. 72-73)

8 Apply clear coat

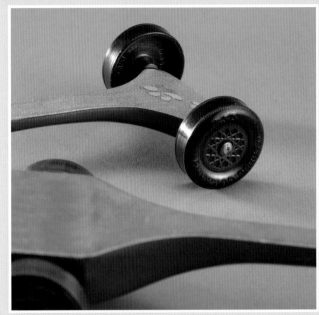

Measured Drawings

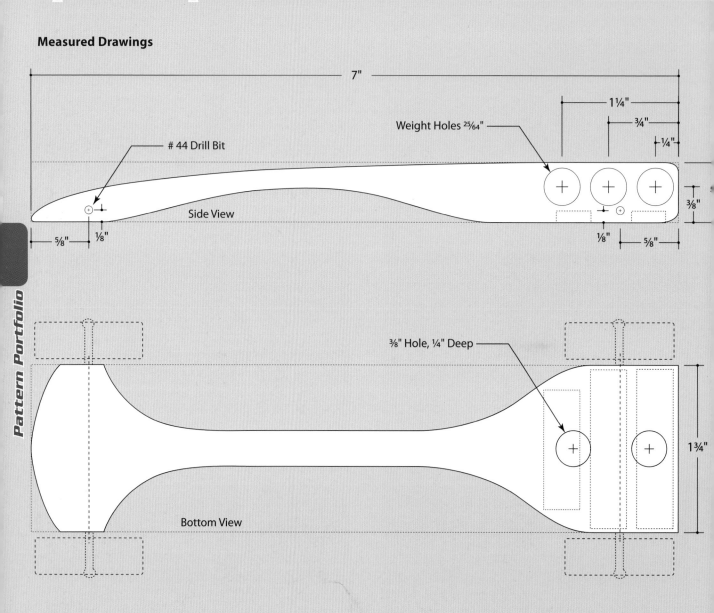

7"

44 Drill Bit

Weight Holes ²⁵⁄₆₄"

1¼"

¾"

¼"

Side View

⅜"

⅝"   ⅛"

⅛"   ⅝"

⅜" Hole, ¼" Deep

1¾"

Bottom View

Cutting Pattern

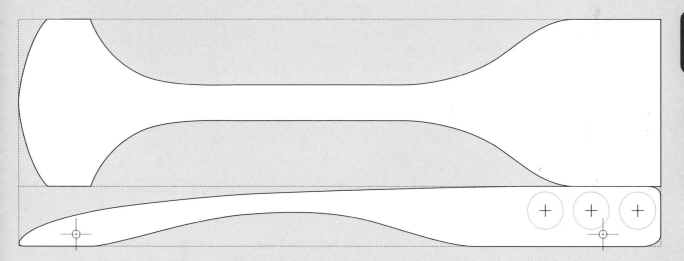

'32 Speedster

Inspired by the hot rods from old car magazines, this advanced pattern has simple, clean lines. The interior looks very difficult to create, but it's actually quite easy. Simply cut out the side profile and attach a ⅜" wooden block to form the cockpit sides. Though a solder windshield and front suspension are shown here, you can create these items just as you did the Vintage Racecar steering wheel on pages 55–56. You can also omit the front suspension and instead create a simple windshield from bent wire. No matter how you build this car, it's sure to be a showstopper.

Quick Tips

1 Flip the block over and drill new axle holes

2 Using the Cockpit Cutting Pattern, cut out the cockpit from the BSA-supplied block

3 Cut the rear wheel well from the side blocks using the Side Block Cutting Pattern

4 Glue the side blocks to the BSA block to form the cockpit sides

5 Cut the side profile and then cut the top profile from the assembled blocks

6 Remove the material above the front axles to form the hood sides

7 Add body filler to form the top of the seat

8 Add the weights and fill in the holes (see pp. 9-11)

9 Sand the entire car smooth

10 Build the windshield and front suspension

11 Paint with the colors of your choice (see pp. 59-74)

12 Apply clear coat

Measured Drawings

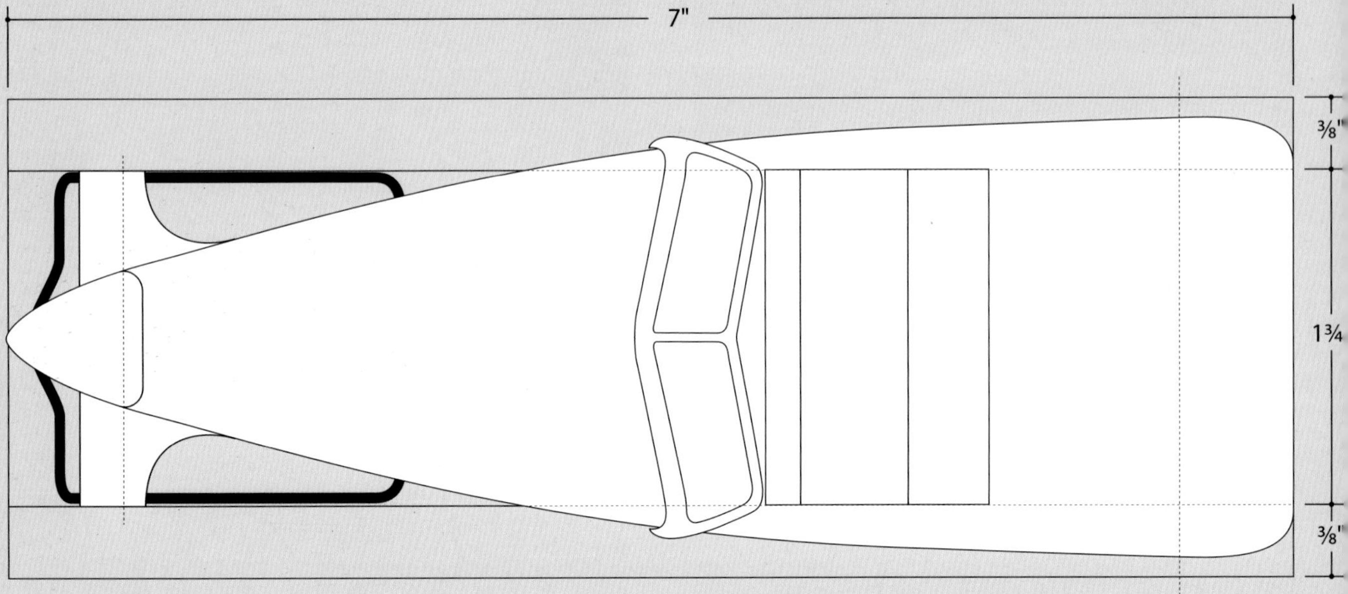

7"

3/8"

1 3/4

3/8"

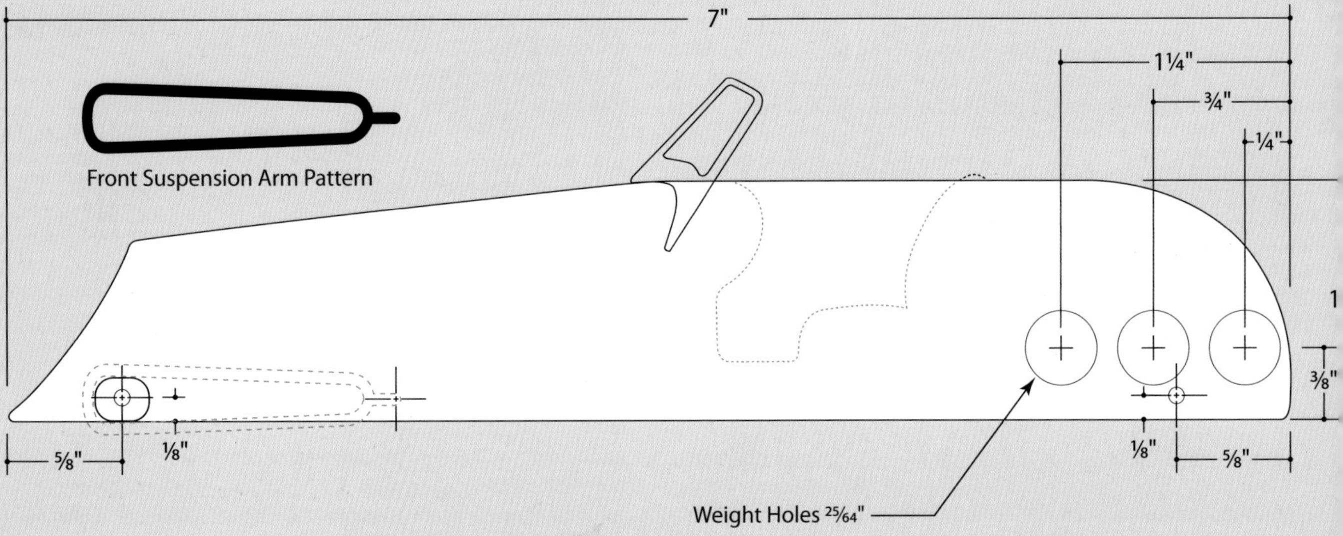

Front Suspension Arm Pattern

7"

1 1/4"

3/4"

1/4"

1

3/8"

5/8"

1/8"

1/8"

5/8"

Weight Holes 25/64"

Cutting Pattern

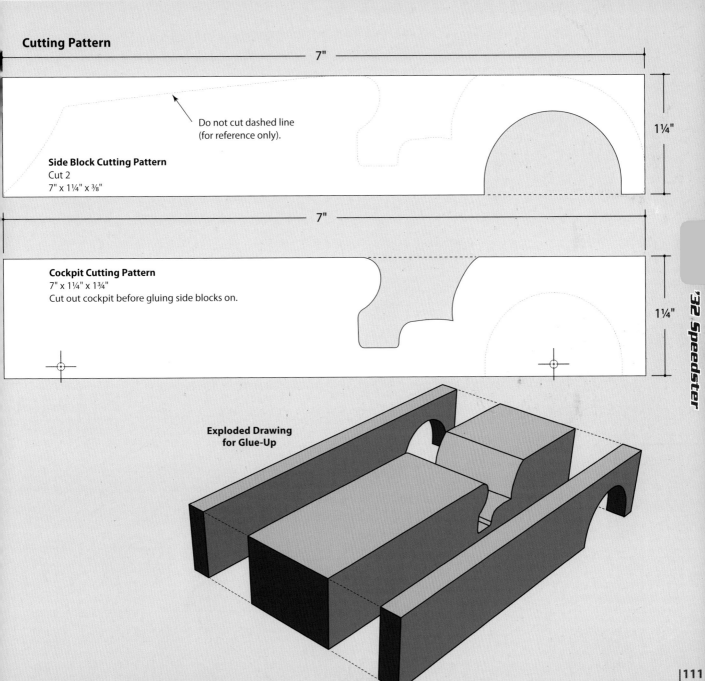

7"

Do not cut dashed line
(for reference only).

Side Block Cutting Pattern
Cut 2
7" x 1¼" x ⅜"

1¼"

7"

Cockpit Cutting Pattern
7" x 1¼" x 1¾"
Cut out cockpit before gluing side blocks on.

1¼"

'32 Speedster

**Exploded Drawing
for Glue-Up**

Wide-Body Racer

My daughter and I built this elegant car to race in the family Pinewood Derby at our pack last year. The car's simplicity and clean lines made it stand out. Pay particular attention to the fenders if you choose this design. They are what set this car apart!

Quick Tips

1 Flip the block over and drill new axle holes or use the BSA-supplied axle slots

2 Cut the wheel wells from the side blocks using the Side Panel Pattern

3 Glue the side blocks to the BSA block

4 Cut the side profile

5 Add the weights and fill in the holes (see pp. 9-11)

6 Sand the entire car smooth

7 Paint with the colors of your choice (see pp. 59-75)

8 Add decals (optional) (see pp. 72-73)

9 Apply clear coat

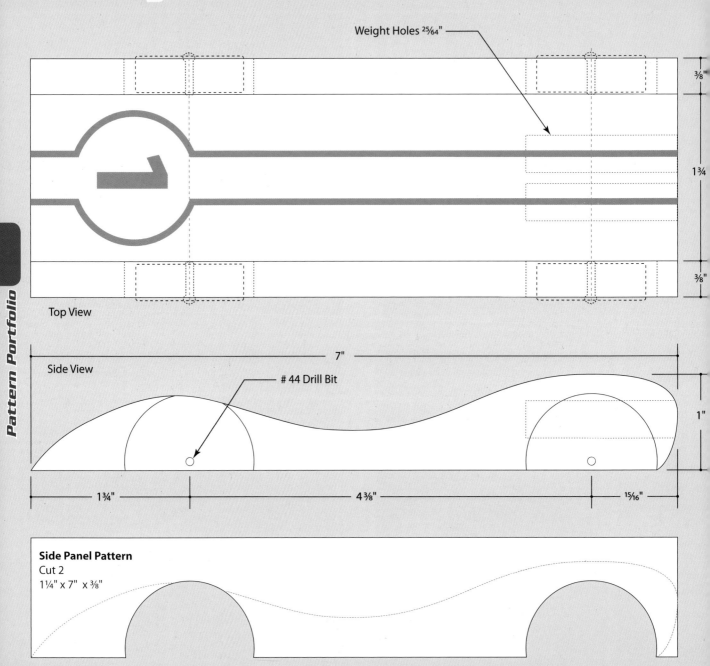

Weight Holes ²⁵⁄₆₄"

$\frac{3}{8}$"

$1\frac{3}{4}$

$\frac{3}{8}$"

Top View

Side View

7"

44 Drill Bit

1"

$1\frac{3}{4}$"

$4\frac{3}{8}$"

¹⁵⁄₁₆"

Side Panel Pattern
Cut 2
$1\frac{1}{4}$" x 7" x $\frac{3}{8}$"

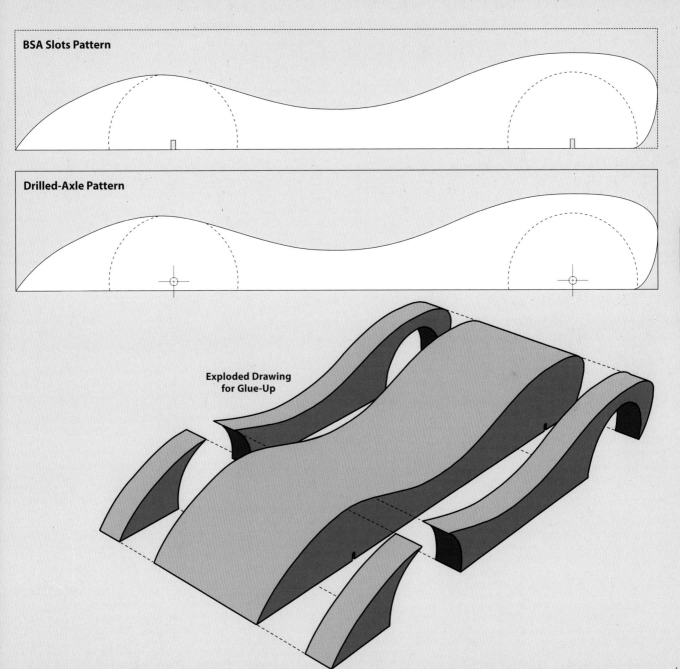

BSA Slots Pattern

Drilled-Axle Pattern

**Exploded Drawing
for Glue-Up**

Blank Patterns

Standard Wheelbase

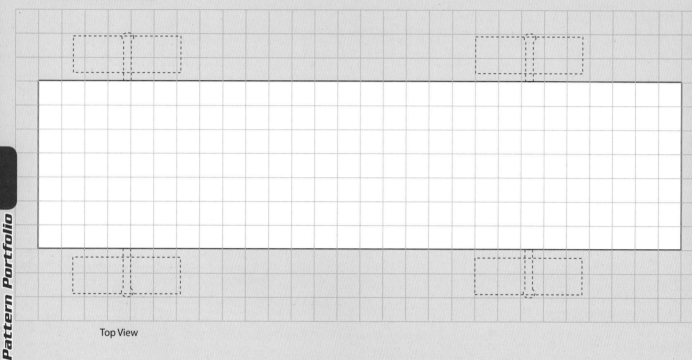

Top View

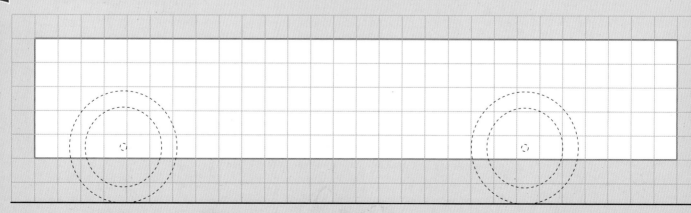

Side View

Extended Wheelbase

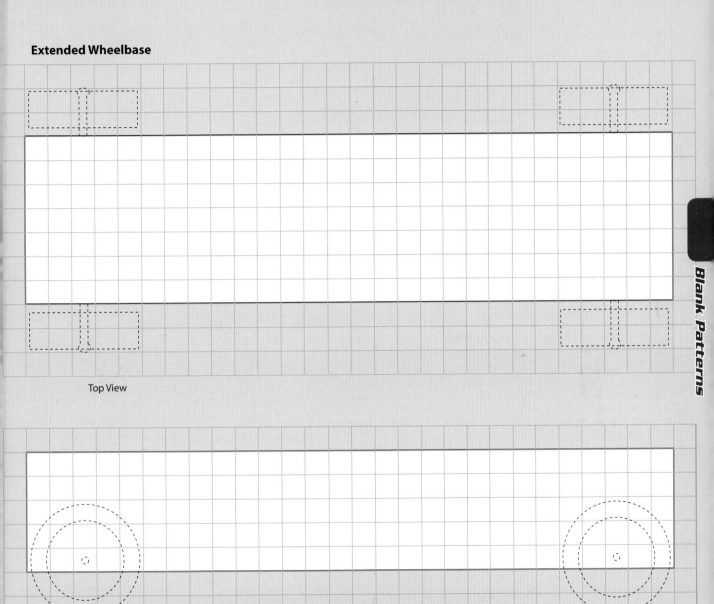

Top View

Side View

Resources

Official Pinewood Derby Supplies
Boy Scouts of America
P.O. Box 7143
Charlotte, NC 28241-7143
1-800-323-0736
www.scoutstuff.org

Book on Pinewood Derby History
Don Murphy
P.O. Box 3881-B
Torrance, CA 90510
(310) 320-4343
www.pinewoodderbystory.com

Rotary/Shaper Tools
Dremel
4915 21st Street
Racine, WI 53406
1-800-437-3635
www.dremel.com

Decal Paper
Papilio
Newark TX USA
(817) 489-5249
www.papilio.com

Model Paints
The Testor Corporation
440 Blackhawk Ave
Rockford, IL 61104
www.testors.com